Study Guide

BUSINESS FINANCIAL MANAGEMENT

FOURTH EDITION

Copyright © 1998
ISBN: 0-9659459-1-X

JLH Enterprises
632 West Wayne Ave.
Wayne, PA 19087

Copyright © 1998 by JLH Enterprises.

Photograph © Index Stock Photography.

Printed by The MACK Printing Group, Science Press Division, Ephrata, Pa 17522.

All rights reserved. No part of this publication may be reproduced or transmitted in any form or by any means, electronic or mechanical, including photocopy, recording, or any information storage and retrieval system, without permission in writing from the publisher.

Requests for permission to make copies of any part of this book should be directed to Managing Editor at JLH Enterprises.

Address Editorial Correspondence

Managing Editor, JLH Enterprises
632 West Wayne Avenue
Wayne, PA 19087

Book Ordering Information

JLH Enterprises
632 West Wayne Avenue
Wayne, PA 10987
Phone: 610-995-0980
FAX: 610-989-0776

ISBN: 0-9659459-1-X

JLH Enterprises

Study Guide

Business Financial Management

Chapter 1	Finance and Business	*1*
Chapter 2	The Financial System	*13*
Chapter 3	Markets for Stocks and Bonds	*29*
Chapter 4	Time Value of Money	*43*
Chapter 5	Risk and Rate of Return	*65*
Chapter 6	Security Valuation	*87*
Chapter 7	Cost of Capital	*101*
Chapter 8	Capital Investments and Cash Flows	*125*
Chapter 9	Evaluating Capital Investments	*143*
Chapter 10	Capital Budgeting and Risk	*161*
Chapter 11	Working Capital Policies	*179*
Chapter 12	Working Capital Practices	*195*
Chapter 13	Analyzing Financial Performance	*229*
Chapter 14	Financial Planning	*253*
Chapter 15	International Financial Management	*273*

1 FINANCE and BUSINESS

OVERVIEW

This chapter provides an introduction to the study of business financial management. It includes a review of certain key business and accounting concepts essential to the understanding of finance. The objective of business financial management, the maximization of shareholder wealth through stock price maximization, is introduced. Every decision facing a financial manager should be addressed with this objective in mind.

OUTLINE

The field of finance can be divided into three main areas: financial markets and institutions, investments, and business financial management.

- Money is the focus of financial markets and institutions. Financial markets match suppliers of money (lenders) with users of money (borrowers). Financial institutions such as commercial banks and the Federal Reserve System facilitate the transfer of funds between the different market players.

- Investments is the study of how people and institutions invest excess funds in securities in order to earn a positive return on their investment. The questions of what to buy, when to buy, and what combination to buy are at the core of the field of investments.

Chapter 1

- Business financial management involves the study of the finance function in a business. Whether the finance department of a company is large or consists of just one person, there are certain fundamental principles and objectives that must be understood in order to make sound financial decisions. (See the text for an organizational chart of a sample finance department for a large company.) This area of finance is the focus of this textbook--an introduction to the basic principles if business financial management.

Businesses can be organized in one of three forms: sole proprietorship, partnership, and corporation.

- A sole proprietorship is a company owned by one person.

- A partnership is a company owned by two or more persons.

- A corporation is an entity created by an agreement between a state and the persons forming the company. It legally exists apart from its owners, unlike the sole proprietorship and the partnership. Although sole proprietorships and partnerships outnumber corporations, corporations have the greatest monetary impact on the U.S. economy.

The advantages of being organized as a corporation include:

- Limited financial liability for the owners, with their losses limited to their investment in the corporation.

- Ease of transfer of ownership of the corporation. *Common stock* is the security representing ownership of a corporation, and it is easier to sell a share of stock than to sell a sole proprietorship or a share of a partnership.

- Corporations have perpetual lives; that is, they continue to exist after the deaths of owners, permitting corporations to obtain long-term financing with maturities that are independent of owners' life expectancies.

One disadvantage of the corporate form of organization is double taxation.

- Corporations pay taxes on income the corporation earns, plus the owners (shareholders) must pay personal income taxes on cash dividends they receive from the corporation. Thus, the same dollar of income may be taxed twice. In contrast, the income earned by a proprietorship or a partnership is taxed at the individual owner's personal tax rate only.

A review of some basic accounting terms and the format of a balance sheet and an income statement will be useful to students at this point.

- **Assets** are items of value that a company owns. Assets are typically divided into current assets and fixed assets. *Current assets* include items such as cash, marketable securities, accounts receivable, and inventory, all items that can be converted into cash within one year. Equipment, buildings, and land are the *fixed assets* of a firm, often referred to as capital assets or productive assets. The amount of a company's assets at a particular point in time can be found by looking at the left-hand side of its balance sheet.

- **Debt** is one form of financing a company's assets. Debt is a promise to repay an amount of money in the future. *Current liability* accounts such as accounts payable, wages payable and taxes payable represent promises to repay within a period of one year. To obtain *long-term financing*, many companies issue notes, bonds or take out mortgages. These varying forms of debt can be seen on the right-hand side of a company's balance sheet.

- **Equity** represents an owner's investment in a company and is the alternative to debt for financing assets. For corporations, equity comes from the sale of stock to investors and through the retention of company earnings (as opposed to distributing them to the owners in the form of cash dividends). The amount of equity a company has at a particular point in time can be found by looking at the right-hand side of the balance sheet under the company's debt.

- **The balance sheet** is a listing of a company's assets, debt, and equity at a point in time, such as the end of a year, the end of a quarter, or the end of a month. Total assets of a company equal debt plus equity, thus the name *balance* sheet (the dollar value of the left-hand side must equal the dollar value of the right-hand side).

- **The income statement** shows a company's earnings over a period of time, and is prepared annually, quarterly, or monthly. The income statement begins with the company's sales revenue and then deducts a series of different costs (expenses) to

Chapter 1

arrive at the company's earnings.

- **Sales** (Total Revenue) represent cash inflows to the company from the sale of goods and services.

- **Cost of goods sold** comprises direct labor costs, raw material costs, and other costs incurred in the production of a product or the provision of a service.

- **Gross profit** equals Sales minus Cost of goods sold.

- **Operating expenses** are the sum of selling expenses and administrative expenses, that is, company expenses not directly associated with the production of a good or service.

- **Earnings before interest and taxes (EBIT)** is also referred to as net operating income. EBIT is calculated by subtracting operating expenses from gross profit.

- **Interest expense** can be deducted from a company's earnings before the company calculates its corporate tax obligation, according to federal tax laws. Any interest paid on short- and long-term debt can be included in interest expense.

- **Earnings before taxes (EBT)** results when interest expense is deducted from EBIT.

- **Taxes** include federal, state and local taxes to which a company is subject.

- **Earnings after taxes (EAT)** is also referred to as net income, profit, or the company's *bottom line*. Students beginning a study of business financial management often assume that the objective of a financial manager is to maximize the company's profit, as measured by earnings after taxes. However, the objective of profit maximization may cause managers to make decisions in the short-term that will be harmful to the company and its owners in the long-run. Because of this and other problems with profit maximization, another objective will be introduced.

The objective of business financial management in a corporation is to maximize shareholder wealth through the maximization of stock price. To maximize stock price, managers must consider the impact of every financial decision on the following factors:

Chapter 1

- The **size of expected cash flows.** Stock price is in part determined by the amount of future cash inflows expected by shareholders. These inflows come in the form of 1) cash dividends and 2) cash from the eventual sale of the stock to another investor.

  The company's potential for paying cash dividends to shareholders depends on the cash flows generated from operations. Large cash flows lead shareholders to expect large cash dividends, and this expectation leads to stock price increases. Thus, in the field of finance, the emphasis is on *cash flow*, not accounting profits. It is possible for a company to show an accounting profit when it has no cash, but it is not possible for a company to pay a cash dividend to its shareholders when there is no cash in the corporate checking account.

  The rate of return from owning a stock *for a one year period* can be calculated as follows (see Chapter 4 for periods longer than one year):

  $$\text{Rate of Return} = \frac{(\text{Selling price} - \text{Buying price}) + \text{Cash Dividends}}{\text{Buying Price}}$$

- The **risk** or uncertainty surrounding the expected cash flows. Most investors do not like uncertainty; they are said to be *risk averse*. Thus, there is a negative or inverse relationship between the amount of perceived risk and stock price.

- The **timing of expected cash flows**. Cash flows expected to be received sooner have a higher value than cash flows expected later because of the *time value of money*. Shareholders prefer to receive cash flows earlier so they can invest the cash and earn a return on it.

With the objective of stock price maximization in mind, the financial manager must make three principal decisions:

- **Investment Decision** - determining what assets the company should own.

- **Financing Decision** - determining how these assets should be financed.

- **Dividend Decision** - determining whether earnings should be paid out as dividends or retained for reinvestment in the company.

Chapter 1

In attending to these tasks, the financial manager should strive to make decisions that tend to:

- Increase the amount of the expected future cash flows.
- Decrease the perceived risk of the cash flows.
- Produce cash flows as soon as possible.

An agency problem can arise if the professionals hired to manage a company do not keep the best interests of the company's owners in mind when making decisions.

- Shareholders can encourage managers to perform in a manner consistent with shareholders' interests by creating appropriate management incentive contracts and by monitoring management activity. The costs associated with these activities are called *agency costs*. Examples include expenditures for auditing financial statements, bonding costs against malfeasance, and executive compensation policies such as executive stock options.

Stakeholders are different groups of people who have stakes in the success of the corporation.

- Stakeholders include customers, suppliers, employees, management, the community, creditors, governments, and shareholders. Working toward the objective of stock price maximization for shareholders requires financial managers to consider and meet the needs of the other stakeholders in the company as well.

GLOSSARY OF KEY TERMS

agency costs: costs arising from the separation of ownership and control of corporations

agency problem: potential conflict of interest between agents (managers) and principals (shareholders)

agent: anyone who acts for another (the principal), with the other's consent

assets: items of value owned by a company

balance sheet: company's statement of financial position at a point in time; a listing of assets and claims against them -- debt and equity

capital structure: mix of long-term debt and equity

cash dividend: distribution of cash from a corporation to its shareholders

common stock: security representing ownership in a corporation

corporation: company formed by legal agreement between the state and the persons establishing the company

debt: money a company owes

dividend decision: process of deciding whether to retain earnings or pay dividends

equity: owner's investment in a company

executive stock options: incentive compensation to executives, enabling them to buy their company's stock in the future at a fixed price

financial structure: mix of all liabilities (current and long-term) and equity

financing decision: process of choosing among alternative sources of financing

funds: cash raised from debt and equity sources

income statement: financial statement detailing a company's earnings for a period of time

inflation: decline in the purchasing power of money measured by an increase in the average price level

investment decision: process of allocating funds for investment in competing assets

maturity: date when repayment is due

optimal capital structure: best combination of long-term debt and equity

partnership: company owned by two or more persons who have entered into an agreement

rate of return: dollar return expressed as a percentage of investment

risk: perceived uncertainty in future cash flows or expected rate of return

risk averse: desiring to avoid risk

sole proprietorship: company owned by one person

stakeholders: groups who gain (or lose) as a company prospers (or fails).

Chapter 1

MULTIPLE CHOICE SELF-TEST

1. The division of finance emphasized in the text is

    a. investments
    b. personal finance
    c. financial markets
    d. financial institutions
    e. business financial management

2. Which of the following is not an advantage of the corporate form of organization?

    a. ease of transfer of ownership
    b. limited liability of owners
    c. dividends are exempt from corporate taxes
    d. ability to raise large amounts of capital from various sources
    e. continuation of the corporation is not dependent on the life expectancy of any one owner or manager

3. Which of the following would not be classified as a current asset?

    a. inventory
    b. accounts receivable
    c. cash
    d. accounts payable
    e. marketable securities

4. Which of the following cannot be deducted from a firm's earnings prior to the calculation of the firm's tax obligation?

    a. dividend payments to shareholders
    b. cost of goods sold
    c. interest payments on outstanding debt
    d. selling and administrative expenses
    e. all of the above are tax deductible

Chapter 1

5. Sources of equity to a corporation include

    a. sale of obsolete assets
    b. development of new products
    c. issuance of corporate bonds
    d. the payment of dividends
    e. sale of stock to investors

6. After purchasing common stock, shareholders may receive cash flows

    a. from dividends
    b. by selling their stock
    c. from their salaries as shareholders
    d. both a and b above
    e. all of the above

7. The key goal of financial managers is to

    a. maximize earnings per share
    b. maximize shareholder wealth
    c. maximize sales revenue
    d. minimize cost of operations
    e. minimize number of shareholders

8. Which of the following is not a principal decision addressed by a financial manager?

    a. dividend decision
    b. investment decision
    c. personnel decision
    d. financing decision
    e. all of the above are principal decisions addressed by a financial manager

Chapter 1

9. The timing of cash flows is important to the price of stock because

   a. a dollar received today can be invested
   b. dollars received in the future are worth more than dollars received today
   c. tomorrow can be forecast with certainty
   d. stockholders do not have much time
   e. patience is unrewarded in the financial markets

10. Because of risk aversion, there is _____ relationship between the degree of uncertainty surrounding cash flows and the firm's stock price.

    a. an inverse
    b. a positive
    c. an uncorrelated
    d. an unidentifiable
    e. a friendly

11. When management is engaged to act on behalf of the shareholders of a firm, it is acting as a(n)

    a. principal
    b. secondary player
    c. agent
    d. proprietor
    e. partner

12. A capital gain from the sale of common stock

    a. is another term for rate of return on investment
    b. is the purchase price minus the selling price
    c. results when no dividends are paid
    d. is usually guaranteed by the corporation
    e. results when selling price exceeds the original purchase price

Chapter 1

PROBLEMS

1. Jane Johnson purchased 100 shares of stock in the Mightymac Corporation for $25 per share. She sold the stock after one year for $35 per share and received a cash dividend of $5 per share immediately before selling. Calculate her rate of return for the one year period.

2. Bob Lease purchased 50 shares of Computerco for $18 per share one year ago. Computerco did not have a good year. The company did not pay dividends and the price has dropped to $15 per share. If Bob sells his shares at this price, what rate of return will he have earned for the one year period?

3. Sharon Sloane purchased 200 shares of ZZZ Sleep Corp. for $50 per share. After one year, the price of the stock has risen to $52.50 per share. The company paid a dividend of $0.50 per share at year end. What is the dollar amount of the capital gain Ms. Sloane will earn if she sells at $52.50?

4. If an investor purchased a share of stock for $10 and sold it one year later for $11, what is the size of cash dividend that the investor must have received if he earned a 20% return on his investment for the one year period?

5. You purchased 100 shares of Calcom Corp. for $22 per share one year ago. Yesterday, the company paid a cash dividend of $0.25 per share. Today, you sell your shares for $23.50 per share. What rate of return did you earn on your one year investment?

SOLUTIONS TO MULTIPLE CHOICE SELF-TEST

1. e 7. b
2. c 8. c
3. d 9. a
4. a 10. a
5. e 11. c
6. d 12. e

Chapter 1

SOLUTIONS TO PROBLEMS

The problems are based on the following formula:

Rate of Return = (Capital gain + Dividend)/Buying Price

1. [($35-$25) + $5]/$25 = $15/$25 = 0.60, or 60%

2. [($15-$18) + $0]/$18 = -$3/$18 = -0.1667, or 16.67% loss

3. ($52.50-$50) = $2.50 per share gain × 200 shares = $500

4. [($11-$10) + x]/$10 = 0.20
   ($11-$10) + x = $2
   $1 + x = $2
   x = $1 dividend

5. [($23.50-$22)+$0.25]/$22 = $1.75/$22 = 0.0795, or 7.95%

2 The FINANCIAL SYSTEM

OVERVIEW

The U.S. financial system transfers funds from savers to users. In return for funds from savers, users issue securities, or claims on future cash flows. Financial markets and financial institutions facilitate this exchange. This chapter examines the various types of financial markets and the securities traded in them. Interest rates on securities are considered and theories are introduced to explain differences in yields on short- and long-term securities. Financial institutions and their changing roles in the financial system are examined to provide students with a comprehensive picture of the environment in which financial managers must work to obtain funding for investments.

OUTLINE

Because of the difficulty users of funds would have in directly identifying and connecting with appropriate savers of funds, financial markets and institutions have been created to facilitate the flow of funds between users and savers.

- Financial markets, also known as *securities markets*, provide a system for issuing stocks, bonds, and other securities. Users issue securities in the financial markets in exchange for funds; savers provide the funds in exchange for the securities.

Chapter 2

- Financial institutions collect funds from savers, giving them claims on future cash flows (securities). These institutions, in turn, provide the funds to users, either through direct loans to users or through the institution's purchase of securities in the financial markets.

Financial markets serve three major functions in the financial system:

- They enable the transfer of large dollar sums collected from thousands of savers to the users of funds.

- They provide liquidity for investors by creating a mechanism for the sale and resale of securities.

- They furnish a target -- stock price -- by which financial managers can measure the success of the company's decisions. Since financial markets, like other markets, are governed by the forces of supply and demand, changes in security prices provide financial managers with readable signals about how shareholders view the company's investment and financing decisions.

There are many separate and sometimes overlapping classifications of financial markets. Financial markets may or may not be an actual place; some markets are networks that facilitate the trading of securities.

- **Primary versus Secondary Markets:** The primary market, also called the *new issues market*, is where securities are issued for the first time. Many firms use *investment bankers* to assist in the sale of new securities to investors. The primary market serves to ease the transfer of funds from savers to users.

- The secondary market is the resale market where investors buy and sell previously issued securities. *Stockbrokers* and *dealers* are active in these markets, trading securities for clients (stockbrokers) or on their own accounts (dealers). The secondary market provides liquidity for outstanding securities and furnishes information to financial managers on stock prices and economic conditions.

- **Debt versus Equity Markets:** Whenever a company, individual, or government issues or sells a debt security like a bond, the transaction takes place in the debt market. Whenever a company or individual issues or sells common stock, the transaction takes

Chapter 2

place in the equity market.

- **Organized Exchanges versus Over-The-Counter (OTC) Markets:** Debt and equity financial markets can be further classified as organized exchanges or over-the-counter markets. An organized exchange is a centrally located trading facility whose members buy and sell securities according to specific exchange rules. The New York Stock Exchange is an example of an organized, secondary, equity market in which the stocks of corporations are traded. The over-the-counter (OTC) market is not a specific location but is rather a decentralized network of brokers and dealers connected electronically by telephones and computers. U.S. government securities are one example of securities traded over-the-counter. Most bond trading occurs over-the-counter.

- **Money versus Capital Markets:** The money market is any place where securities with a maturity of one year or less are traded. The capital market is any place where securities with a maturity greater than one year are traded.

The money market is used (1) to issue short-term debt securities to raise funds to finance temporary increases in assets and (2) to invest temporarily excess cash in money market securities.

- All money market securities share the following characteristics: (1) are debt securities; (2) have short-term (one year or less) maturities; (3) have low *default risk* (the chance the issuer will not be able to pay interest and principal); and (4) usually offer relatively low expected rates of return compared with capital market securities.

The largest part of the money market is the market for U.S. Treasury bills (T-bills).

- T-Bills are issued with maturities of 13, 26, or 52 weeks; the smallest denomination available for purchase is $10,000.

- T-bills do not pay a stated dollar interest but instead are sold at a discount from face value. When the T-bill matures, the investor receives the full face value. Dealers quote information about T-bill prices in the financial press using discount yields.

Other types of money market securities include commercial paper, negotiable certificates of deposit, banker's acceptances, and federal funds.

Chapter 2

- *Commercial paper* is issued by companies to raise large amounts of funds for a short time period. Maturities on commercial paper generally range from 30 to 270 days, and it is sold in large denominations, with $1 million being commonplace. Like T-bills, commercial paper trades at a discount from face value. Since investors perceive a higher risk in commercial paper than in T-bills, the rate of return on commercial paper is higher than on T-bills.

- A *negotiable certificate of deposit* is a claim on funds deposited at a commercial bank, issued in denominations of $100,000 or larger. They are issued for a specified number of days at a specified interest rate, and are traded in the secondary market among securities dealers. These should not be confused with the certificates of deposit offered to individual investors by banks, savings and loan associations, and credit unions.

- A *banker's acceptance* is a time draft that has been accepted (guaranteeing payment) by a bank, usually in connection with the financing of imported goods. They trade in the secondary market at a discount from face value.

- *Federal funds* are excess reserves at commercial banks that can be loaned to other banks having reserve deficiencies. Financial managers watch the interest rate charged on federal funds for clues to changes in monetary policy.

Long-term securities, such as bonds and common stock, are traded in the capital market.

- Capital market securities have several characteristics that distinguish them from money market securities:

    Capital market securities include both debt and equity securities.

    The maturity of capital market securities ranges from one year to infinity. For example, common stock never matures.

    The risk of capital market securities varies from low to extremely high.

    Because of their higher risk and longer maturity, capital market securities usually must offer rates of return that exceed those on money market securities.

Chapter 2

The issuers of securities in the capital market include the U.S. Treasury, U.S. Agencies, state and local governments, and corporations.

- *Treasury notes* have maturities of ten years or less; *Treasury bonds* have maturities longer than ten years. Both notes and bonds pay semiannual interest.

- Some U.S. Agencies issue their own securities. For example, the Government National Mortgage Association issues securities nicknamed *Ginnie Maes* and the Federal Home Loan Mortgage Corporation issues *Freddie Macs* as a way of raising funds for certain government mortgage programs.

- State and local governments issue bonds called municipal bonds. The interest investors receive on municipal bonds is exempt from federal taxation. State taxation of municipal bonds varies from state to state.

Corporate securities trading in the capital market include bonds, common stock, and preferred stock.

- Most **corporate bonds** have a $1,000 denomination and pay interest semiannually. The amount of interest is determined by the *coupon rate* on the bond. The interest paid to bondholders is tax deductible for the corporation.

    Corporate bonds include an *indenture* which is a contract describing the issuer's obligations to its bondholders. *Protective covenants* are clauses in an indenture that state specific rights of bondholders. A *trustee*, usually a trust company or commercial bank, is assigned the duties of protecting the rights of the bondholders.

    Corporate bonds come in many varieties, including *secured* bonds (those backed by pledged assets) and *unsecured* bonds (backed only by the faith and credit of the issuing company). Examples of different types of bonds include:

    1) *Mortgage Bonds* - backed by pledged real property (plant, land, buildings).
    2) *Collateral Trust Bonds* - backed by securities (stocks or bonds) kept by trustee.
    3) *Equipment Trust Certificates* - backed by equipment such planes or locomotives.
    4) *Debentures* - backed only by the issuer's promise to pay.
    5) *Subordinated Debentures* - debentures whose claims come after other debentures.
    6) *Deep-Discount Bonds* - bonds with a market price far below par value.

Chapter 2

    7) *Floating-Rate Bonds* - pay interest that varies with prevailing market rates.
    8) *Junk Bonds* - high-risk, high-yield bond often associated with leveraged but-outs.
    9) *Income Bonds* - bonds that pay interest only if company has sufficient earnings.
    10) *Put bonds* - bonds that allow bondholder to sell (put) the bond back to company.

- **Common stock** does not carry any obligation for the company to pay dividends. Dividends that are paid come out of after-tax earnings, like preferred stock dividends.

Closely held companies are owned by only a few shareholders, while *publicly held companies* are owned by a large and diverse group of shareholders.

Common shareholders are residual claimants, meaning they are last to be paid when earnings are distributed. The maximum number of shares a corporation can issue, as stated in the company charter, is the *authorized stock*. The total number of shares held by shareholders is *outstanding stock*, while *treasury stock* are shares repurchased by the issuing corporation.

Common shareholders have certain rights, including the right to transfer their ownership, receive information on company operations, attend annual shareholders' meetings, and be exposed to limited liability from company creditors. In most cases stockholders have the right to elect the board of directors. Stockholders also sometimes have the right of *proxy* (empowering some else to vote on their behalf) and a *preemptive right* (the right of first refusal on purchase of additional shares of common stock issued by the company).

- **Preferred stock** pays a stated, constant dividend that investors expect will continue forever. Thus, it is considered a *perpetuity*. Preferred stockholders must receive their dividends before common stockholders can receive any dividends. Preferred dividends are paid out of after-tax earnings.

- From the *investor's point of view*, bonds offer the least risk because interest on bonds is a legal obligation and must be paid. Common stock offers the most risk because there is no guarantee that investors will ever receive dividends or that stock price will rise above purchase price. Preferred stock falls in between bonds and common stock in terms of risk to the investor.

- From the *issuing company's perspective*, bonds represent the most risk because the company can be sued by the bondholders if it misses scheduled interest payments. Common stock is the least risky way of raising long-term funds because there is no legal obligation for the company to pay common stock dividends. Again, preferred stock falls in the middle in terms of risk to the issuing company.

The level of interest rates in general is impacted by Federal Reserve actions and government deficits.

- The Federal Reserve's purchase and sale of U.S. Treasury securities to control the money supply causes changes in interest rate levels.

- The issuance of government securities to finance the federal deficit also impacts on the general level of interest rates.

The interest rate on a *particular* security depends on the risk, liquidity, and maturity of the security.

- Higher risk leads investors to require a higher rate of return as compensation for bearing the higher risk.

- Securities that have less liquidity must pay higher interest rates in order to attract purchases.

- Generally, the shorter the maturity, the lower the interest rate, as is seen in the difference between money market securities and capital market securities. However, investor attitudes toward the maturity of debt securities are complex.

The relationship among interest rates on debt securities that differ only in maturity is known as the term structure of interest rates.

- *Yield curves* provide graphic portrayals of interest rates plotted against varying maturities of securities that have the same level of risk and liquidity.

- Upward-sloping yield curves, indicating that long-term securities carry higher interest rates than short-term securities, have occurred most frequently in past years.

- Yield curves can also be downward-sloping, humped, or flat.

Chapter 2

Economists have developed three theories to explain the shape of the yield curve.

- The *liquidity preference theory* postulates that long-term rates are higher than short-term rates because investors prefer liquidity and therefore are willing to accept lower interest rates on short-term securities. Issuers of debt securities prefer long-term financing in order to avoid frequent refinancings. Thus, issuers willingly pay higher rates of interest on long-term bonds than on short-term bonds.

- The *market segmentation theory* states that the interest rate on securities in a specific maturity range is determined by the supply of and demand for securities within that range. Short-term interest rates are determined by the supply of short-term funds compared to the demand for short-term funds. The same holds true for the long-term market segment and the intermediate-term market segment. The market segmentation theory could conceivably explain any shape of the yield curve.

- The *expectations theory* argues that long-term interest rates depend on investors' expectations about future short-term interest rates because investors purchase short- and long-term securities to maximize the *average* rate of return over a planned investment period. The long-term rate today is the average of the expected short-term rates for that long-term time period.

For example, suppose investors expect short-term (1-year) rates to be 4%, 5%, 6%, and 7% over the next four years. The rate today on a security that will mature in 4 years would be (4+5+6+7)/4, or 5.5%. Long-term rates (5.5% on a 4-yr. security) will be higher than short-term rates (4% on a 1-yr. security) when investors expect short-term rates to rise in the future. An upward-sloping yield curve will result.

In contrast, suppose investors had expected short-term rates to be 7%, 6%, 5%, and 4%, respectively, over the next four years. The rate today on a 4-yr. security would be (7+6+5+4)/4, or 5.5%, just like in the example above. However, when compared to today's 1-yr. rate of 7%, the 5.5% 4-yr. rate is lower, resulting in a downward-sloping yield curve. This will occur when investors expect future short-term rates to falling.

Financial institutions can be classified as depository or nondepository.

- Depository institutions accept checkable deposits (accounts on which depositors may write checks) and use funds deposited to make loans. Examples include commercial banks, savings and loan associations, savings banks, and credit unions.

■ Nondepository institutions do not accept checkable deposits and exist to provide a particular financial service to their customers. Examples include insurance companies, pension funds, mutual funds and closed-end investment companies. Mutual funds and closed-end investment companies both offer investors the advantage of professional management of funds and the reduction of risk through investing in a diversified portfolio.

■ The character of financial institutions has changed greatly in the past decade due in large part to the government deregulation of financial institutions that took place during the 1980s. Historical differences among financial institutions have decreased while competition among them has increased.

GLOSSARY OF KEY TERMS

acceleration of maturity: principal of a bond becomes immediately payable if the issuer violates terms of the indenture
authorized stock: maximum number of shares of stock a corporation may issue
banker's acceptance: credit instrument issued by an importer's bank that guarantees payment of an exporter's invoice
callability: right of a bond issuer to redeem bonds before maturity at a stated cash price
capital market: financial market where securities with a maturity greater than one year are traded
charter: contract with a state establishing a corporation's existence
checkable deposits: accounts on which depositors may write checks
closely held company: company with few shareholders
collateral trust bond: bond secured with securities of other companies
commercial paper: short-term promissory notes issued by corporations
coupon rate: promised rate of interest on a bond
cumulative dividend: preferred stock whose missed dividends accumulate from year to year
dealer: company (or individual) that buys and sells securities for its own account
debenture: unsecured bond

Chapter 2

debt market: financial market where debt securities such as bonds are traded

deep-discount bond: bond with a market price far below par value

default risk: uncertainty surrounding a debtor's ability to pay interest and principal

depository institution: financial institution that accepts deposits and loans funds

direct placement: issuing securities directly to savers in return for funds, bypassing all middlemen

discount yield: discount percentage from face value based on a 360-day year; used for quoting yields on T-bills

dividends in arrears: prior-period dividends presently payable by a company

equipment trust certificate: bond secured with mobile equipment--railroad cars, trucks or planes

equity market: financial market where common stock is traded

federal funds: excess reserves at commercial banks that can be loaned to other banks having reserve deficiencies

financial institution: commercial bank or other organization that collects funds from savers and makes loans to users

financial intermediary: financial institution that creates new securities as it serves as a middleman between savers and users of funds

financial market: mechanism for facilitating the issuance of securities; also known as the securities market

floating rate bond: bond with a coupon rate that changes with a market interest rate

income bond: bond that pays interest contingent on the company's level of earnings

indenture: bond contract describing the issuer's obligations to its bondholders

investment banking firm: organization that specializes in the distribution of corporate securities to investor-savers

investment yield: the expected rate of return on T-bills and other securities sold at a discount from face value

issued stock: authorized shares distributed to investors

junk bond: bond with high default risk and high expected return

liquidity: ease with which securities can be converted into cash with little or no loss in current value

monetary policy: action by the Federal Reserve System to control the money supply and interest rates

money market: financial market where securities with a maturity of one year or less are traded

mortgage: long-term IOU collateralized with (backed by) real estate

mortgage bond: bond secured with real property--plant, land, and buildings

negotiable certificate of deposit: claim on funds deposited at a commercial bank, issued for a specified number of days at a specified interest rate

open-market operations: Federal Reserve purchase and sale of U.S. Treasury securities to control the money supply

organized exchange: coordinated, centrally located trading facility whose members buy and sell securities

outstanding stock: issued shares in the hands of shareholders

over-the-counter (OTC) market: decentralized, electronically connected network of brokers and dealers

perpetuity: security that investors expect will pay a level dollar amount forever

portfolio: collection of securities

preemptive right: shareholder's right of first refusal on the purchase of additional shares of common stock issued by the company

primary market: financial market where securities are first issued

protective covenant: clause in an indenture guaranteeing specific rights to bondholders

proxy: document empowering someone else to vote on behalf of a shareholder

proxy fight: competition among groups for the proxies of shareholders

publicly held company: company with many shareholders

put bond: bond that gives the holder the option to sell (put) the bond back to the issuer at the face value before maturity

secondary market: financial resale market where investors buy and sell previously issued securities

security: documentary evidence of claims on future cash flows -- stocks, bonds, and other promises to pay

stock certificate: document evidencing corporate ownership

stockbroker: company (or individual) that executes customer orders to buy or sell securities

subordinated debenture: unsecured bond with a claim secondary to those of specified other creditors

term structure of interest rates: relationship between yields and maturities of debt securities

treasury stock: issued shares repurchased by the issuing corporation

trustee: legal representative of bondholders who ensures that the issuer does not violate the terms of the indenture

yield curve: graph of yields on debt securities of differing maturities

Chapter 2

MULTIPLE CHOICE SELF-TEST

1. An individual (or company) who buys and sells securities for his or her own account (as opposed to buying and selling on behalf of customers) is called a(n)

    a. investment banker
    b. stockbroker
    c. dealer
    d. money manager
    e. government trader

2. Financial markets include all of the following except

    a. primary market
    b. money market
    c. debt market
    d. OTC market
    e. all of the above are financial markets

3. Funds can be transferred from savers to users

    a. through the financial markets
    b. by a financial intermediary
    c. by direct placement of securities
    d. all of the above
    e. none of the above

4. Money markets are important for the transfer of

    a. foreign currency
    b. gold bullion
    c. stocks
    d. short-term funds
    e. capital assets

Chapter 2

5. Which of the following is not characteristic of money market securities?

    a. are all debt securities
    b. have long-term maturities
    c. have low default risk
    d. usually offer low rate of return compared with capital market securities
    e. all are characteristic of money market securities

6. The largest part of the money market is the market for

    a. U.S. Treasury bills
    b. federal funds
    c. certificates of deposit
    d. commercial paper
    e. dollars

7. Which of the following is a capital market security?

    a. T-bills
    b. commercial paper
    c. negotiable certificate of deposit
    d. banker's acceptance
    e. preferred stock

8. Which of the following will cause the interest rate on a security to be high?

    a. a relatively small degree of risk
    b. illiquidity
    c. a very short maturity
    d. low interest rates in general
    e. a readily available resale market

Chapter 2

9. The general level of interest rates will rise if

    a. the Federal Reserve sells T-bills
    b. the federal government borrows to finance a growing deficit
    c. the economy is experiencing inflation
    d. the money supply decreases
    e. all of the above

10. Long-term rates should be higher than short-term rates because lenders prefer the safety of liquid instruments, and borrowers prefer to avoid the expenses of frequent refinancings. This theory is known as

    a. liquidity preference theory
    b. Federal Reserve policy theory
    c. market segmentation theory
    d. yield curve theory
    e. expectations theory

11. The expectations theory of interest rates helps to explain why

    a. short-term rates and long-term rates are equally stable
    b. short-term rates are more stable than long-term rates
    c. short-term rates are more volatile than long-term rates
    d. short-term rates and long-term rates are equally volatile
    e. none of the above

12. Nondepository financial institutions include all of the following except

    a. insurance companies
    b. pension funds
    c. money market funds
    d. savings banks
    e. closed-end investment companies

Chapter 2

PROBLEMS

1. The current 1-year rate is 4% and the current 2-year rate is 4.5%. Based on the expectations theory, what does the market expect the 1-year rate to be one year from now?

2. According to the expectations theory, if investors expect the 1-year rates to be as follows: Year 1 = 8%; Year 2 = 7%; Year 3 = 6.5%; Year 4 = 6%; what is the current rate on a *3-year* security?

SOLUTIONS TO MULTIPLE CHOICE SELF-TEST

1. c   7. e
2. e   8. b
3. d   9. e
4. d   10. a
5. b   11. c
6. a   12. d

SOLUTIONS TO PROBLEMS

1. 4.5% = (4% + x%)/2
    9% = 4% + x
    x = 5%

2. x = (8% + 7% + 6.5%)/3
    x = 7.17%

Chapter 2

3 MARKETS for STOCKS and BONDS

OVERVIEW

In order to raise funds, companies sell new stocks and bonds in the primary market. This chapter provides an overview of government regulation of the primary market and the process by which companies issue new securities. After the securities are issued, they are traded in the secondary market, so regulation of the secondary market is examined as well. Organized exchanges and the over-the-counter market are looked at in some detail, and stock and bond price quotations in the financial press are explained. Since the prices of individual stocks are affected by the general level of prices in the securities markets, measurements of price behavior are introduced so students will have a better understanding of what these indicators convey.

OUTLINE

Government regulation of the primary market began with the passage of The Securities Act of 1933, which requires disclosure of all relevant information pertaining to a new securities issue.

- Before issuing new securities, companies are required to file a *registration statement* with the Securities and Exchange Commission (SEC). The registration statement contains detailed information about the issuing firm, which the SEC will review to make sure the firm has fully disclosed all information investors need to make a decision about purchasing the security.

Chapter 3

- Prospective buyers must be given a *prospectus* before they purchase a new security. The prospectus is a condensation of the registration statement and is distributed after SEC approval has been received.

- While awaiting SEC approval, the issuing firm may distribute a preliminary prospectus called a *red herring* to stimulate interest in the security issue. The red herring is much like the final prospectus except that it does not include the purchase price of the security, which cannot be released until SEC approval has been granted.

- Once SEC approval has been granted, an advertisement in the financial press, referred to as a *tombstone*, announces the availability of the new issue.

Several types of securities are exempt from the federal registration requirement.

- These include intrastate issues, commercial paper, small issues, issues regulated by other federal commissions, issues of charities and non-profit organizations, and U.S. government, federal agency, state and local government issues. Intrastate issues are subject to state regulations called *blue sky laws*.

The SEC allows companies to register all of the new security issues they expect to offer over a two-year period with one registration statement. This is called a shelf-offering.

- When the firm is ready to issue all or part of the registered securities, they can do so quickly by filing a short-form statement. Shelf-offerings reduce paperwork and issuance costs, and managers can be ready to issue the securities when market conditions are favorable.

Companies often engage the services of investment bankers to assist in the issuance of new securities. Investment bankers should not be confused with commercial bankers; they do not take deposits or make loans. Investment banking firms assist the issuers of securities in four ways:

- *Origination*: Investment bankers advise financial managers on the type of security to issue, the timing of the offering, and the pricing of the security. They also help prepare the registration statement for the SEC and the prospectus for investors.

- *Underwriting*: Investment bankers will buy the entire issue of new securities from the issuing company in anticipation of reselling them to investors for a higher price. Underwriting transfers the risk of unsold securities from the issuing company to the investment banking firm.

- *Syndication*: For large offerings, investment banking firms will join together in a syndicate to underwrite the securities, thereby spreading the risk of unsold securities.

- *Distribution*: The investment bankers, or the syndicate, will sell the issue directly to investors or to a *selling group* composed of dealers and other investment bankers who, in turn, sell to investors.

Companies must choose between public offerings of new securities or private placement.

- When an issue is privately placed, the securities are sold directly to investors. This method is commonly used to sell bonds and preferred stock to institutional investors and to sell new common stock to current shareholders. Firms may employ investment bankers to locate institutional purchasers or to serve as *standby underwriters*, who will sell unsold shares of common stock to the public.

- No SEC registration is required with private placements, and issuance costs are lower than that of public offerings because of lower marketing costs. However, the interest or dividend rate offered on the new securities is normally higher because of the low liquidity of private placement issues.

Public offerings are issued through investment bankers by negotiated sale or competitive-bid.

- Under the negotiated sale, the issuing company and the investment banking firm come to an agreement on the securities to be issued, the timing of the sale, and the fee for services. The investment bankers may underwrite the issue or sign a *best-efforts agreement*, in which they promise to use their best efforts to sell the securities. Under a best-efforts agreement, the issuing company keeps any unsold securities.

- Securities issued using a competitive-bid process are sold to the highest bidder (investment banker), who underwrites, syndicates and distributes the issue. Origination

Chapter 3

services are not a part of a competitive-bid.

Flotation costs are the costs of issuing new securities. They consist of the underwriting spread and the expenses of the issuing firm.

- The underwriting spread is the difference between the securities' market value (selling price to investors × the number of shares sold) and the proceeds to the issuing company (what the investment bankers pay to buy the issue). The underwriting spread is in essence the underwriter's fee, or gross profit.

- The issuing company incurs many expenses besides the cost of the investment bankers. These include legal, printing and engraving, accounting, and other miscellaneous expenses.

- Total flotation costs are the sum of the underwriting spread and the various expenses of the issuing company.

After securities are issued by companies in the primary market, they are traded among investors in the secondary market. The Securities Exchange Act of 1934 requires disclosure of information in the secondary market. It also established the Securities and Exchange Commission (SEC) to enforce regulations in both the primary and the secondary markets.

- Companies listed on organized exchanges (and some in the OTC market) must file periodic reports with the SEC. Form 10-K, consisting of detailed audited financial statements and information on company operations, must be filed annually. Unaudited quarterly financial statements must be filed on Form 10-Q. Corporate insiders must submit monthly reports of their holdings and transactions in an attempt to deter *insider trading* (using confidential information to make profits from trading in the company's stock). Organized exchanges must also register with the SEC.

Generally, the stocks of larger corporations trade on an organized exchange such as the New York Stock Exchange (NYSE) or the American Stock Exchange (AMEX).

- To be listed on an organized exchange, firms must pay a listing fee and meet several listing requirements. Organized exchanges rely on *auction trading*, with stock shares selling to the highest bidder. Brokers send buy and sell orders from investors to representatives of the brokerage firm on the trading floor. The order is taken to the trading post where the stock trades, and the trade is made with another broker or with a *specialist*, who makes a market in a specific stock by standing ready to buy or sell when no one else will.

- Investors pay brokerage commissions when buying or selling securities. Stocks are often sold in *round lots*, blocks of 100 shares, but trades may also be made in *odd lots* (one to 99 shares) at a slightly higher commission.

Stock price quotations are published daily for stocks listed on various exchanges. Most stocks are quoted in eighths of a dollar; 1/8 is $0.125.

- Stock quotations can be used to calculate some other measures of company performance. For example, the P-E ratio (price-earnings) ratio can be used to calculate the latest annual *earnings per share (EPS)* of a listed company.

    P-E ratio = price per share/earnings per share

    Since the P-E ratio and the closing price per share are published, EPS can be easily derived from them.

- Likewise, the P-E ratio and the dividend yield can be used to calculate the *dividend payout ratio*, which measures the percentage of earnings paid out as common stock dividends.

    Dividend payout ratio = Dividend yield × P-E ratio

    The dividend payout ratio indicates the company's ability to continue paying the dividend indicated in the stock quotation. High ratios create concern, while low ratios provide assurance to investors.

The over-the-counter market is a nationwide network of thousands of securities dealers and brokerage firms who make a market for stocks not listed on an organized exchange.

- The National Association of Securities Dealers (NASD) licenses dealers and supervises trading procedures. OTC stock price quotations in the financial press are provided by

Chapter 3

NASDAQ, the National Association of Securities Dealers Automated Quotations.

Most corporate bonds trade over-the-counter. The New York Stock Exchange does list some bonds, and quotations of these bond prices can be found in the financial press. However, many corporate bonds never trade in the secondary market.

- Initial buyers of corporate bonds often hold them until maturity. Additionally, institutional investors such as insurance companies and pension funds sometimes trade bonds privately among themselves, so these trades would not be reflected in bond price quotations.

Individual stock prices tend to rise and fall in step with the overall stock market. Financial managers need to be aware of overall market movements to determine the impact on their company's stock.

- The general level of common stock prices is affected by investors' expectations about economic growth and stability. In a *bull market*, investors are confident about the economy, and stock prices are increasing in general. When investors lose confidence and expect a recession or a depression, stock prices in general decline, which is referred to as a *bear market*.

To monitor movement in the stock market, financial managers follow certain market indicators, such as the Dow Jones Industrial Average and the Standard & Poor's 500 Index.

- The Dow Jones Industrial Average (DJIA) is a popular stock market indicator composed of 30 industrial common stocks. The DJIA is not an arithmetic average of 30 stock prices (the Dow had at one point risen above 8000, which could not be the average price per share of any 30 stocks!). Because the component stocks change from time to time, the divisor used in computing the DJIA is adjusted so that changes in composition do not change the index.

- The Standard & Poor's 500 Index consists of 500 common stocks and is considered more representative of the overall stock market than the DJIA. The S&P 500 compares the total market value of the 500 stocks with their base established during 1941-1943.

- Although the DJIA and the S&P 500 are different in composition, they both react similarly to market expectations about economic growth and stability. With both indexes, the actual level of the index is not nearly as important to financial managers as the day to day percentage change in the index.

GLOSSARY OF KEY TERMS

bear market: period of falling stock prices

best-efforts agreement: agreement between the investment banker and securities-issuing corporation that the banker will serve only as a broker for a new issue

blue sky laws: state laws regulating securities issued and sold within state borders

bull market: period of rising stock prices

competitive-bid procedure: process in which the issuer sells its securities to the highest-bidding investment banker

current yield: rate of return on a bond based on dollar interest but ignoring changes in bond prices

distribution: marketing a new issue of securities to investors

dividend payout ratio: percentage of a company's earnings paid out as dividends on common stock; dividends per share divided by earnings per share

dividend yield: percentage return on stock price based solely on dividends; dividends per share divided by price per share of stock

Dow Jones Industrial Average (DJIA): stock price average of a group of 30 industrial companies

Eurobonds: bonds sold outside the country in whose currency they are denominated

Eurodollars: U.S. dollars on deposit in banks outside the country of the currency's origin

flotation costs: all costs associated with issuing new securities

foreign bonds: bonds sold and denominated in one country, by an issuer from another country

initial public offering (IPO): issuing a type of security (e.g., common stock) for the first time

negotiated sale: agreement between the investment banker and securities-issuing corporation on services and fee

odd lot: fewer than 100 shares of a stock

Chapter 3

origination: planning a new issue of securities through negotiations between the investment banker and the issuing corporation

price-earnings (P-E) ratio: price investors pay for $1 of a company's earnings per share; earnings multiple; price per share divided by earnings per share

prospectus: abridged version of the registration statement, giving investors information relevant to the purchase of securities

red herring: preliminary prospectus given to potential buyers of securities prior to SEC approval of the issue

registration statement: detailed financial and operating information filed with the SEC about a company

round lot: block of 100 shares of a stock

Securities Act of 1933: federal law requiring a company to register its new issues of securities with the Securities and Exchanges Commission

Securities Exchange Act of 1934: federal law governing activities in the secondary market

Securities and Exchange Commission: federal agency that regulates U.S. financial markets

shelf offering: offering of new securities during a 24-month period whose registration is covered by a single Form S-1

specialist: stock exchange member who makes a market in a specific stock

Standard & Poor's 500 Index (S&P 500): stock price index of 500 industrial, utility, transportation, and financial corporations

standby underwriting: agreement between the investment banker and securities-issuing corporation that the banker will buy all unsold shares of a new issue for resale

stock market: financial market for trading stock; any place that stock trades in the secondary market

syndication: temporary banding together of investment bankers to share the risk of issuing new securities

tombstone: advertisement announcing a new issue of securities

underwriting: guaranteeing proceeds from a new issue of securities by buying the entire issue for resale

underwriting spread: difference between the market value of the security and the proceeds to the company

Chapter 3

MULTIPLE CHOICE SELF-TEST

1. Laws regulating the issue of new securities exist

    a. at the state level
    b. at the federal level
    c. at both state and federal levels
    d. only for bonds, not stocks
    e. only for stocks, not bonds

2. Regulation by the SEC focuses on

    a. money market securities
    b. long-term securities issued across state lines
    c. only debt securities
    d. long-term securities sold intrastate
    e. only equity securities

3. Which of the following was not a part of The Securities Act of 1933?

    a. a registration statement must be filed with the SEC
    b. a prospectus must be given to potential investors
    c. a 10-K must be filed annually with the SEC
    d. public disclosure of all relevant information
    e. all of the above were a part of the 1933 Act

4. An advertisement in the financial press announcing a new issue of securities is called

    a. registration statement
    b. shelf-offering
    c. best-efforts announcement
    d. blue herring
    e. tombstone

Chapter 3

5. Investment bankers will perform all of the following except

    a. preparation of the registration statement
    b. provision of low interest, long term loans to companies for investment purposes
    c. advisement on type of security to issue
    d. underwriting of the issue
    e. preparation of the prospectus

6. Companies may raise funds by issuing securities

    a. which are placed directly with institutional investors
    b. to an underwriter who will resell them to the public
    c. through an investment banker, who promises his best efforts to sell them to the public
    d. to its existing shareholders in the form of a rights offering, with or without a standby underwriting agreement
    e. in any of the above ways

7. The largest part of the flotation costs is the

    a. underwriting spread
    b. market value decline
    c. proceeds
    d. printing expense
    e. legal fees

8. The percentage of earnings available to common stockholders paid out as dividends is measured by the

    a. dividend yield
    b. dividend payout ratio
    c. quarterly dividend
    d. P-E ratio
    e. current yield

Chapter 3

9. The Securities and Exchange Commission was established by the

    a. Securities Act of 1933
    b. Securities Exchange Act of 1934
    c. Insider Trading Act of 1941
    d. New York Stock Exchange
    e. National Association of Securities Dealers

10. Both stock and bond quotations in *The Wall Street Journal* contain

    a. 52-week high and low prices
    b. amount of dividends paid
    c. closing price for the day
    d. opening price for the day
    e. face value of the security

11. Which of the following is not characteristic of corporate bonds?

    a. face value is normally $1,000
    b. interest is normally paid semiannually
    c. many bonds are sold through private placement
    d. initial purchasers of bonds often hold them until maturity
    e. dividends are normally paid quarterly

12. A period of falling stock prices is called a

    a. bear market
    b. bull market
    c. short market
    d. marginal market
    e. transactional market

39

Chapter 3

PROBLEMS

1. TXR, Inc. has issued one million shares of common stock, which sold to investors for $5.50 per share. If the underwriting spread is $0.75 per share and TXR's accounting, legal, printing and engraving expenses amount to $250,000, what are total flotation costs as a percentage of gross proceeds?

2. BT&T Communications recently paid its common shareholders a $0.45 per share quarterly dividend. The closing price of BT&T stock yesterday was $24.00 and the latest earnings per share available to common shareholders was $2.00. Calculate BT&T's dividend yield, P-E ratio, and dividend payout ratio.

3. Kiwi Computers' stock trades over-the-counter. Bid and asked prices are currently 12 3/4 and 13 1/4, respectively. You contact your broker to sell your 500 shares of Kiwi. If the broker's commission is $100, how much do you net from the sale?

4. Effron Oil has bonds outstanding that are currently priced at 104. Bondholders receive interest payments of $30 every six months. Calculate Effron's current yield.

SOLUTIONS TO MULTIPLE CHOICE SELF-TEST

1. c   7. a
2. b   8. b
3. c   9. b
4. e   10. c
5. b   11. e
6. e   12. a

Chapter 3

SOLUTIONS TO PROBLEMS

1. Gross proceeds = 1,000,000 shares × $5.50 = $5,500,000

   Underwriting spread = 1,000,000 shares × $.75 = $750,000

   $750,000 underwriting spread + $250,000 other expenses = $1,000,000 total flotation costs

   $1,000,000/$5,500,000 = 18.2%

2. Dividend yield = Annual dividend/Price per share
   = ($0.45 × 4)/$24.00
   = 0.075, or 7.5%

   P-E ratio = Price per share/Earnings per share
   = $24.00/$2.00
   = 12

   Dividend payout ratio = Dividend yield × P-E ratio
   = 7.5% × 12
   = 90%

3. Gross proceeds = $12.75 × 500 shares = $6,375
   Net proceeds = $6,375 - $100 commission = $6,275

4. Current yield = Annual interest/closing price
   = ($30 × 2)/(104% × $1,000)
   = $60/$1,040
   = 0.0577, or 5.77%

Chapter 3

4 TIME VALUE of MONEY

OVERVIEW

In Chapter One, the financial management objective of stock price maximization was introduced. The determinants of stock price were said to be the size, timing, and risk of expected cash flows. This chapter concentrates on the *timing* of cash flows. Because money can be invested to earn a return, cash flows received or paid at different points in time have different values. This concept, *the time value of money*, is based on standard mathematical relationships between the present value and future value of cash flows. Chapter Four presents techniques financial managers can use to value cash flows occurring at different times.

OUTLINE

Money has time value because a dollar received today is worth more than a dollar received tomorrow.

- Cash on hand can be invested to earn a return or it can be used for current consumption. To induce individuals to loan money and forgo consumption, borrowers must promise to pay a return that is greater than the individuals' *opportunity cost*. Opportunity cost is the best return an alternative use of the funds would provide.

Chapter 4

Calculating the future value of a cash investment requires compounding, and the process is called future-value analysis.

■ Most loans involve *compound interest*, where interest is earned on both the original principal and the interest accumulated to date. In contrast, *simple interest* involves payment of interest on the principal only.

To calculate the future value of a starting amount using compound interest, the mathematical equation is

$$FV = PV(1+i)^n$$

FV = future value at the end of *n* periods (e.g., years)
PV = present value, or the beginning dollar amount
i = compound interest rate per period (e.g., per year)
n = number of periods separating the future and present values

■ For example, suppose you invest $1,000 in a savings account paying 6 percent interest per year and want to know what the account value will be in 5 years:

$$FV = PV(1+i)^n = \$1,000(1.06)^5 = \$1,338.23$$

Contrast that amount with what would be in the account if simple interest were involved:

$$\$1,000 + (\$1,000 \times 0.06 \times 5 \text{ years}) = \$1,300.00$$

The $38.23 difference between the two balances represents the interest earned on the accumulated interest over the 5 years. Again, note that compound interest is much more prevalent than simple interest and is the basis for future-value analysis.

Future value can also be calculated using the interest factor equation.

$$FV = PV(FVIF_{i,n})$$

where $FVIF_{i,n}$ is the *future-value interest factor* equivalent to $(1+i)^n$ from the mathematical equation above. Tables are published that contain values of FVIF for various values of *i* and *n*.

- For example, in Appendix A.1 in the textbook, $FVIF_{6\%,5}$ = 1.3382. The future value in the savings account 5 years from now at 6 percent interest would be $1,000 × 1.3382 = $1,338.20. Because of rounding, answers using the interest factor equation sometimes vary a little from those calculated using the mathematical equation.

A third method for computing future values is using a financial calculator.

- Financial calculators permit the direct entry of the values for PV, *i*, and *n*, computing the value for FV. The owner's manual of your financial calculator will show you how to use your calculator for future and present value computations.

Calculating the present value (today's value) of a future cash flow requires discounting, and the process is called discounted-cash-flow (DCF) analysis, or present-value analysis.

- Discounting a future value to the present time is the reverse of compounding a present value to a future time.

The mathematical equation for future value can be solved for present value, yielding the following present value equation:

$$PV = FV(1+i)^{-n}$$

- For example, suppose you can earn 8 percent per year on a 4-year certificate of deposit. How much money must you invest today to have $2,000 at the end of 4 years?

$$PV = FV(1+i)^{-n} = \$2,000(1.08)^{-4} = \$1,470.06$$

The equation using interest factors to calculate present value is

$$PV = FV(PVIF_{i,n})$$

where $PVIF_{i,n}$ is the *present-value interest factor* equivalent to $(1+i)^{-n}$ from the mathematical equation above. Appendix A.2 in the textbook contains PVIF for various combinations of *i* and *n*. In the previous example, the PVIF for 4 periods at 8 percent

Chapter 4

interest would be 0.7350, yielding a present value of $2,000 \times 0.7350 = \$1,470.00$.

In financial decision making, cash flows may occur periodically and vary in amount over time. The present value of an uneven series of cash flows is calculated by summing the present values of the individual cash flows. The general equation for calculating the present value of an uneven series of cash flows is

$$PV = C_1(1+i)^{-1} + C_2(1+i)^{-2} + \ldots + C_n(1+i)^{-n}$$

where $C_0, C_1, C_2, \ldots, C_n$ represent cash flows occurring at different times.

- For example, find the present value of the following cash flows using a discount rate of 9 percent:

End of Year	Cash Flow
0	-$15,000
1	+ 6,000
2	+ 7,000
3	+ 9,000

Notice that (-) cash flows represent cash outflows, or investments, and (+) cash flows represent cash inflows, or returns. Time period zero refers to the present; thus, this example involves an initial cash investment of $15,000 and returns of $6,000, $7,000 and $9,000 over the next three years.

$$PV = -\$15,000 + \$6,000(1.09)^{-1} + \$7,000(1.09)^{-2} + \$9,000(1.09)^{-3}$$

$$= -\$15,000 + \$5,504.59 + \$5,891.76 + \$6,949.65 = \$3,346.00$$

The future value of an uneven series of cash flows is determined by summing the future values of the individual cash flows. Caution must be used in determining the number of periods each cash flow earns interest.

- For example, suppose you make the following deposits in your bank account:

Chapter 4

End of Year	Cash Flow
0	$500
1	$550
2	$600
3	$650

If the bank pays 5 percent interest, how much will be in your account at the end of 3 years?

$$FV = \$500(1.05)^3 + \$550(1.05)^2 + \$600(1.05)^1 + \$650(1.05)^0$$
$$= \$578.81 + \$606.38 + \$630.00 + \$650.00$$
$$= \$2{,}465.19$$

Note that the $650 deposited at the end of year 3 has not yet had an opportunity to earn interest.

An annuity is an even series of cash flows, constant in amount, that occur at regular fixed periods of time (e.g., years or months).

■ An *ordinary annuity* has cash flows occurring at the end of each period. An *annuity due* has payments occurring at the beginning of each period. Because ordinary annuities are so common in finance, the term *annuity* is used as shorthand for ordinary annuities. The cash flows occurring in an annuity are referred to as payments (PMT), even when they involve the receipt of cash and not the payment of it.

The future value and present value of annuities can be determined using mathematical equations, interest factor equations, and financial calculators.

■ Since financial calculators tend to vary on the required keystrokes for annuities, you should consult the reference guide accompanying your calculator to determine the correct procedure for your calculator.

The mathematical equation for calculating the future value of an ordinary annuity is

$$FVA = PMT \times [(1+i)^n - 1]/i$$

FVA = future value of an ordinary annuity
PMT = payments, or amount of cash flow

Chapter 4

  i = compound interest rate per period
  n = number of periods

■ For example, suppose you deposit $2,000 at the end of each year for the next 40 years. If you can earn 7 percent annual compound interest, how much will you have accumulated by the end of 40 years?

$$FVA = \$2{,}000 \times [(1.07)^{40}-1]/0.07 = \$2{,}000(199.6351120) = \$399{,}270.22$$

Note that the equation takes into account the fact that the last deposit earns no interest.

The interest factor equation for calculating the future value of an ordinary annuity is

$$FVA = PMT(FVIFA_{i,n})$$

where $FVIFA_{i,n}$ is the *future-value interest factor of an annuity* equivalent to $[(1+i)^n-1]/i$ in the mathematical equation above. In Appendix A.3, the FVIFA for 7 percent and 40 periods is 199.64. In the example above, the 40 annual deposits of $2,000 will grow to $399,280.00 at 7 percent interest ($2,000 × 199.64). Rounding of the interest factors in the tables again accounts for the discrepancy in the mathematical and interest factor solutions.

Since the payments in an annuity due occur at the beginning of a period, they earn interest for one more period than a comparable ordinary annuity. To calculate the future value of an annuity due:

$$FVA(Due) = PMT(FVIFA_{i,n})(1+i)$$

■ Multiplying the future-value interest factor of an ordinary annuity by $(1+i)$ accounts for the extra period of compounding in an annuity due. The $FVIFA_{i,n}$ can be determined using the mathematical equation or the interest factor table and can then be adjusted for use with an annuity due.

The mathematical equation for calculating the present value of an ordinary annuity is

$$PVA = PMT \times [1-(1+i)^{-n}]/i$$

PVA = present value of an ordinary annuity
PMT = payments, or amount of cash flows
i = discount rate, or compound interest rate per period
n = number of periods

■ For example, suppose you win a contest and are presented with two options: (1) you can have $75,000 in cash now, or (2) you can receive $10,000 at the end of each year for the next 10 years. Someone who does not understand the time value of money might choose option #2, thinking that 10 payments of $10,000 ($100,000 in total) are better than $75,000 now. However, the ten payments must be adjusted to reflect the fact that they are spread out over ten years. If the relevant discount rate is 10 percent, the present value of the ten payments would be

$$PVA = \$10{,}000 \times [1-(1.10)^{-10}]/0.10$$

$$= \$10{,}000(6.144567106) = \$61{,}445.67$$

Option #1 of $75,000 has the higher present value and should be chosen. If the relevant discount rate had been 5 percent instead of 10 percent, the present value of the ten payments would have been $77,217.35, making option #2 the better deal.

The interest factor equation for calculating the present value of an ordinary annuity is

$$PVA = PMT(PVIFA_{i,n})$$

where $PVIFA_{i,n}$ is the *present-value interest factor of an annuity* equivalent to $[1-(1+i)^{-n}]/i$ in the mathematical equation above. Appendix A.4 shows a PVIFA of 6.1446 for 10 periods at 10 percent, giving a PVA of $10,000 × 6.1446 = $61,446.00.

The present value of an annuity due is larger than the present value of the comparable ordinary annuity because payments occur at the beginning of each period, not the end. To calculate the present value of an annuity due:

$$PVA(Due) = PMT(PVIFA_{i,n})(1+i)$$

Multiplying the present-value interest factor of an ordinary annuity by $(1 + i)$ accounts

Chapter 4

for the payments occurring one period earlier in the annuity due. The $PVIFA_{i,n}$ can be determined by using the mathematical equation or the interest factor table and can then be adjusted for use with an annuity due.

- When a loan is to be repaid with equal, periodic payments, the amount borrowed is considered the PVA. The gradual repayment of the loan is called *amortization*. A *loan amortization schedule* shows the timing of the payments and the breakdown of each payment into interest and repayment of principal.

A perpetuity is an annuity with an infinite life; that is, the payments go on forever. The present value of a perpetuity (PVP) is

$$PVP = PMT/i$$

- For example, if the required rate of return (discount rate) is 8 percent on a perpetuity paying $50 annually, the present value of the perpetuity is $50/0.08 = $625.00. This equation assumes that payments occur at the end of each period. If the payments occur at the beginning of each period, the equation must be modified to account for the payment at time zero:

$$PVP = PMT/i + PMT$$

Notice that since a perpetuity produces payments forever, the future value of a perpetuity is a meaningless concept because there is no stopping point in the future.

Frequency of compounding indicates how often compound interest is paid or earned on principal plus accumulated interest. When the compounding period is less than one year, both the future value and present value equations must be modified.

- To modify the equations for a single cash flow, multiply the number of years, n, by the number of times per year that compounding occurs, m. The interest rate is then divided by m.

The future value equation for a single cash flow with frequent compounding is

$$FV = PV(1 + i/m)^{mn}$$

Chapter 4

- Consider the example from the beginning of the chapter outline, where the future value of $1,000 invested for 5 years at 6 percent compounded annually was found to be $1,338.23. Suppose interest had been compounded quarterly instead of annually:

$$FV = \$1{,}000(1 + 0.06/4)^{4\times5} = \$1{,}000(1.015)^{20} = \$1{,}346.86$$

- The quarterly compounding resulted in a higher future value than the annual compounding. *More frequent compounding is preferred by depositors because their money grows at a faster rate.*

The present value equation for a single cash flow with frequent compounding is

$$PV = FV[1+(i/m)]^{-mn}$$

- In general, more frequent compounding leads to smaller present values. *Borrowers prefer less frequent compounding because they receive larger loans (PV = amount of loan) for a given future payment.*

The nominal annual rate is a stated interest rate that does not reflect frequency of compounding. The effective annual rate is the nominal annual rate adjusted for the frequency of compounding; it is a percentage per year compounded annually. To calculate the effective annual rate from the nominal rate, the following formula is used:

$$\text{Effective annual rate} = (1 + i/m)^m - 1$$

where i is the nominal, or stated, annual rate and m is the number of times compounding occurs in one year.

- For example, the effective annual rate of 10 percent compounded semiannually is

$$\text{Effective annual rate} = (1 + .10/2)^2 - 1 = 0.1025, \text{ or } 10.25\%$$

For a given nominal rate, the more frequent the compounding, the higher the effective annual rate.

An organized approach is useful in solving time value of money problems. Plotting

Chapter 4

the cash flows on a time line is often helpful in understanding the timing of cash flows. Once a time line has been constructed, the following steps should be taken:

(1) Determine whether the problem involves a single cash flow, an uneven series of cash flows, or an annuity.

(2) The second issue to be determined is whether the problem involves future value or present value (or both in complex problems). The information given must be scrutinized to determine whether the known cash flow represents a starting value (PV), an ending value (FV), a series of repayments of a starting value (PVA), or a series of payments accumulating to a future value (FVA).

(3) Once the determinations have been made concerning single cash flows versus annuities, and future value versus present value, the appropriate mathematical or interest factor equation can be selected for solving the problem, or a financial calculator may be used.

■ You should remember that there are four variables in each of the basic time value of money equations, and you may be required to solve for any one of the variables: FV, PV, i, n, FVA, PVA, or PMT. The problem must be studied carefully to determine which variable is missing.

Chapter 4
GLOSSARY OF KEY TERMS

amortize: provide for the gradual repayment of a loan

annuity: even series of cash flows, constant in amount, that occur at fixed intervals, such as years or months

annuity due: annuity in which the payments occur at the beginning of each period

compound interest: interest paid or earned on the principal of a loan *and* on interest accumulated during prior periods

compounding: calculating the future value of a present cash flow

discount rate: percentage used in discounting future cash flows; rate of return that measures the time value of money

discounting: calculating the present value of a future cash flow

effective annual rate: a rate per year compounded annually; the nominal rate adjusted for frequency of compounding

frequency of compounding: frequency with which interest is accumulated; e.g., an annual rate of 8 percent compounded quarterly accumulates interest every 3 months

future-value interest factor: future value of $1 earning *i* percent interest for *n* periods; $FVIF_{i,n} = (1 + i)^n$

loan amortization schedule: table showing the timing of payments necessary to amortize a loan, and the breakdown of each payment into interest and repayment of principal

nominal annual rate: a stated rate per year that compounds more frequently than once per year; e.g., 8 percent per year compounded daily

ordinary annuity: annuity in which the payments (cash flows) occur at the end of each period

perpetuity: security that investors expect will pay a level dollar amount forever

present-value interest factor: present value of $1 due in *n* periods discounted at *i* percent per period; $PVIF_{i,n} = (1 + i)^{-n}$

simple interest: interest paid or earned on the principal of a loan but *not* on interest accumulated during prior periods

Chapter 4

REVIEW OF KEY FORMULAS

Compounding

    Single cash flow $FV = PV(1+i)^n$

    Ordinary annuity $FVA = PMT \times [(1+i)^n - 1]/i$

Discounting

    Single cash flow $PV = FV(1+i)^{-n}$

    Ordinary annuity $PVA = PMT \times [1-(1+i)^{-n}]/i$

    Perpetuity $PVP = PMT/i$

Effective Annual Rate

    Effective Annual Rate $EAR = (1+i/m)^m - 1$

MULTIPLE CHOICE SELF-TEST

1. Money has time value because

    a. no one has enough time
    b. if you wait to receive money, you are able to buy more
    c. if you have money, you can buy time
    d. the future is uncertain
    e. a dollar today is worth more than a dollar tomorrow

Chapter 4

2. The process of calculating the present value of a future cash flow is called

   a. compounding
   b. future-value analysis
   c. ordinary annuity
   d. annuity due
   e. discounted-cash-flow analysis

3. The payment of interest on principal only is called

   a. compound interest
   b. simple interest
   c. principal interest
   d. discount interest
   e. future interest

4. The present value of a future cash flow can be calculated using a(n)

   a. mathematical equation
   b. interest factor table
   c. financial calculator
   d. all of the above
   e. none of the above

5. The quantity $(1 + i)^n$ is the general numerical expression for a(n)

   a. present-value interest factor
   b. future-value interest factor
   c. present-value interest factor of an annuity
   d. future-value interest factor of an annuity
   e. amortization rate

Chapter 4

6. If the present-value interest factor is known, which of the these can be calculated?

   a. present value of a single cash flow
   b. future value of a single cash flow
   c. future-value interest factor
   d. all of the above
   e. none of the above

7. The interest rate in present-value problems is known as the

   a. discount rate
   b. required rate of return
   c. present rate
   d. a and b
   e. all of the above

8. Which of the following represents an even series of cash flows, constant in amount, that occur at regular fixed periods of time?

   a. annuity
   b. ordinary annuity
   c. annuity due
   d. deferred annuity
   e. all of the above

9. The difference between an ordinary annuity and an annuity due is

   a. An ordinary annuity involves a cash inflow and an annuity due involves a cash outflow
   b. An ordinary annuity involves a cash outflow and an annuity due involves a cash inflow
   c. An ordinary annuity is a routine (expected) stream of cash and an annuity due is an unexpected stream of cash
   d. An ordinary annuity has payments that occur at the end of a period and an annuity due has payments that occur at the beginning of a period
   e. An ordinary annuity has payments that occur at the beginning of a period and an annuity due has payments that occur at the end of a period

Chapter 4

10. A table showing the timing of payments necessary to pay off a loan and the breakdown of each payment into interest and repayment of principal is called a(n)

    a. annuity due schedule
    b. ordinary annuity schedule
    c. loan amortization schedule
    d. present-value interest factor table
    e. future-value interest factor table

11. The more frequent the compounding for a given nominal interest rate and a given investment amount

    a. the greater the future value
    b. the greater the present value
    c. the slower the funds accumulate
    d. the lower the effective annual rate
    e. the larger the payment required for a given future value

12. One type of time value of money problem involves determining an annual rate of growth. In this case, you are solving for which of the following variables?

    a. FV
    b. PV
    c. i
    d. n
    e. all of the above

Chapter 4

PROBLEMS

1. At your birth, your parents put $1,000 into an account that pays 6 percent annual interest. Assuming no other deposits, how much is in the account 20 years later?

2. What is the present value of $7,500 to be received at the end of five years with a discount rate of 13 percent per year?

3. You plan to make annual deposits into a savings account that pays 7 percent annual interest according to the following schedule:

End of year	Deposit
0	$1,000
1	$1,250
2	$1,500
3	$1,750

    How much will be in the account at the end of year 3?

4. Find the present value of the following cash stream using an annual discount rate of 14 percent.

End of year	Cash flow
1	$ 5,000
2	$ 7,000
3	$ 8,000
4	$10,000

5. If you deposit $10,000 into an account that pays 5 percent per year compounded daily, how much will you have accumulated at the end of 15 years?

6. Find the present value of $250,000 to be received at the end of thirteen years. Use a discount rate of 9 percent per year compounded semiannually.

Chapter 4

7. You deposit $500 at the end of each year into an account that pays 10 percent annual interest compounded annually. How much will be in the account at the end of 25 years?

8. You have been awarded a grant that will pay you $25,000 per year for the next five years. Payments occur at the end of the year. If your required rate of return is 15 percent per year, what lump sum will you accept today in lieu of the annual payments?

9. To accumulate $100,000 by the time you retire in 40 years at age 62, what is the required annual deposit into an account paying annual interest of 9 percent compounded annually?

10. If you retire at age 62 with $100,000 in a retirement account and continue to earn 9 percent annual interest, what equal amount can you withdraw each year so that by the end of 20 years (age 82), the account balance is zero?

11. If you invest $200 of your salary at the end of each quarter into an account paying 12 percent annual interest compounded quarterly, what will be the value of your account at the end of 1 year?

12. You obtain a $20,000, 5-year loan to buy a new car. The annual interest rate is 12 percent compounded monthly. What will be your monthly payment?

13. Z Rocks Company's stock was priced at $2 per share in 1963. Thirty years later, the stock was selling for $102 per share. What is the compound annual rate of growth of the stock?

14. You borrow $10,000 from your parents and intend to repay it in five annual installments of $2,183.55. What compound annual rate of interest are your parents charging you?

Chapter 4

SOLUTIONS TO MULTIPLE CHOICE SELF-TEST

1. e   7. d
2. e   8. e
3. b   9. d
4. d   10. c
5. b   11. a
6. d   12. c

SOLUTIONS TO PROBLEMS

Mathematical Equation   Interest Factor Equation

1. FV = $PV(1+i)^n$ FV = $PV(FVIF_{i,n})$
       = $\$1{,}000 \times (1.06)^{20}$ = $\$1{,}000(FVIF_{6\%,20})$
       = $\$1{,}000 \times 3.20714$ = $\$1{,}000(3.2071)$
       = $\$3{,}207.14$ = $\$3{,}207.10$

2. PV = $FV(1+i)^{-n}$ PV = $FV(PVIF_{i,n})$
       = $\$7{,}500 \times (1.13)^{-5}$ = $\$7{,}500(PVIF_{13\%,5})$
       = $\$7{,}500 \times 0.542759$ = $\$7{,}500(0.5428)$
       = $\$4{,}070.70$ = $\$4{,}071.00$

Chapter 4

Mathematical Equation	Interest Factor Equation

3. $FV = PV(1+i)^n$ $\qquad\qquad\qquad$ $FV = PV(FVIF_{i,n})$

$FV_0 = \$1,000 \times (1.07)^3$ $\qquad\qquad$ $FV_0 = \$1,000(FVIF_{7\%,3})$
$ = \$1,000 \times 1.22504$ $\qquad\qquad = \$1,000(1.2250)$
$ = \$1,225.04$ $\qquad\qquad\qquad = \$1,225.00$
$FV_1 = \$1,250 \times (1.07)^2$ $\qquad\qquad$ $FV_1 = \$1,250(FVIF_{7\%,2})$
$ = \$1,250 \times 1.1449$ $\qquad\qquad = \$1,250(1.1449)$
$ = \$1,431.13$ $\qquad\qquad\qquad = \$1,431.13$
$FV_2 = \$1,500 \times (1.07)^1$ $\qquad\qquad$ $FV_2 = \$1,500(FVIF_{7\%,1})$
$ = \$1,500 \times 1.07$ $\qquad\qquad = \$1,500(1.0700)$
$ = \$1,605.00$ $\qquad\qquad\qquad = \$1,605.00$
$FV_3 = \$1,750 \times (1.07)^0$ $\qquad\qquad$ $FV_3 = \$1,750(FVIF_{7\%,0})$
$ = \$1,750 \times 1.0$ $\qquad\qquad = \$1,750(1.0)$
$ = \$1,750.00$ $\qquad\qquad\qquad = \$1,7500.00$
$FV = \$1,225.04 + \$1,431.13$ $\qquad$ $PV = \$1,225.00 + \$1,431.13$
$ + \$1,605.00 + \$1,750.00$ $\qquad + \$1,605.00 + \$1,750.00$
$ = \$6,011.17$ $\qquad\qquad\qquad = \$6,011.13$

4. $PV = FV(1+i)^{-n}$ $\qquad\qquad\qquad$ $PV = FV(PVIF_{i,n})$

$PV_1 = \$5,000 \times (1.14)^{-1}$ $\qquad\qquad$ $PV_1 = \$5,000(PVIF_{14\%,1})$
$ = \$5,000 \times 0.87719$ $\qquad\qquad = \$5,000(0.8772)$
$ = \$4,385.96$ $\qquad\qquad\qquad = \$4,386.00$
$PV_2 = \$7,000 \times (1.14)^{-2}$ $\qquad\qquad$ $PV_2 = \$7,000(PVIF_{14\%,2})$
$ = \$7,000 \times 0.76946$ $\qquad\qquad = \$7,000(0.7695)$
$ = \$5,386.27$ $\qquad\qquad\qquad = \$5,386.50$
$PV_3 = \$8,000 \times (1.14)^{-3}$ $\qquad\qquad$ $PV_3 = \$8,000(PVIF_{14\%,3})$
$ = \$8,000 \times 0.67497$ $\qquad\qquad = \$8,000(0.6750)$
$ = \$5,399.77$ $\qquad\qquad\qquad = \$5,400.00$
$PV_4 = \$10,000 \times (1.14)^{-4}$ $\qquad\qquad$ $PV_4 = \$10,000(PVIF_{14\%,4})$
$ = \$10,000 \times 0.59208$ $\qquad\qquad = \$10,000(0.5921)$
$ = \$5,920.80$ $\qquad\qquad\qquad = \$5,921.00$
$PV = \$4,385.96 + \$5,386.27$ $\qquad$ $PV = \$4,386.00 + \$5,386.50$
$ + \$5,399.77 + \$5,920.80$ $\qquad + \$5,400.00 + \$5,921.00$
$ = \$21,092.80$ $\qquad\qquad\qquad = \$21,093.50$

Chapter 4

Mathematical Equation

Interest Factor Equation

5. $FV = PV \times (1+i/m)^{mn}$
    $= \$10,000 \times (1+0.05/365)^{365 \times 15}$
    $= \$10,000 \times (1.000136986)^{5,475}$
    $= \$10,000 \times 2.116891$
    $= \$21,168.91$

6. $PV = FV \times (1+i/m)^{-mn}$
    $= \$250,000 \times (1+0.09/2)^{-2 \times 13}$
    $= \$250,000 \times (1.045)^{-26}$
    $= \$250,000 \times 0.318402$
    $= \$79,600.62$

7. $FVA = PMT \times [(1+i)^n - 1]/i$ $FVA = PMT(FVIFA_{i,n})$
    $= \$500 \times [(1.10)^{25} - 1]/0.10$ $= \$500(FVIFA_{10\%,25})$
    $= \$500(98.34706)$ $= \$500(98.347)$
    $= \$49,173.53$ $= \$49,173.50$

8. $PVA = PMT \times [1-(1+i)^{-n}]/i$ $PVA = PMT(PVIFA_{i,n})$
    $= \$25,000 \times [1-(1.15)^{-5}]/0.15$ $= \$25,000(PVIFA_{15\%,5})$
    $= \$25,000 \times 3.352155$ $= \$25,000(3.3522)$
    $= \$83,803.88$ $= \$83,805.00$

9. $FVA = PMT \times [(1+i)^n - 1]/i$ $FVA = PMT(FVIFA_{i,n})$
    $\$100,000 = PMT \times [(1.09)^{40} - 1]/0.09$ $\$100,000 = PMT(FVIFA_{9\%,40})$
    $\$100,000 = PMT(337.8824)$ $\$100,000 = PMT(337.88)$
    $PMT = \$295.96$ $PMT = \$295.96$

10. $PVA = PMT \times [1-(1+i)^{-n}]/i$ $PVA = PMT(PVIFA_{i,n})$
    $\$100,000 = PMT \times [1-(1.09)^{-20}]/0.09$ $\$100,000 = PMT(PVIFA_{9\%,20})$
    $\$100,000 = PMT \times 9.128546$ $\$100,000 = PMT(9.1285)$
    $PMT = \$10,954.65$ $PMT = \$10,954.70$

Chapter 4

Mathematical Equation

11. $FVA = PMT \times [(1+i)^n - 1]/i$
    $= \$200 \times [(1.03)^4 - 1]/0.03$
    $= \$200(4.18363)$
    $= \$836.73$

12. $PVA = PMT \times [1-(1+i)^{-n}]/i$
    $\$20,000 = PMT \times [1-(1.01)^{-60}]/0.01$
    $\$20,000 = PMT \times 44.95504$
    $PMT = \$444.89$

13. $FV = PV \times (1+i)^n$
    $\$102 = \$2 \times (1+i)^{30}$
    $51 = (1+i)^{30}$
    $51^{1/30} = 1+i$
    $1.14 = 1+i$
    $i = 14\%$

14. $PVA = PMT \times [1-(1+i)^{-n}]/i$
    $\$10,000 = \$2,183.55 \times [1-(1+i)^{-5}]/i$
    $4.5797 = [1-(1+i)^{-5}]/i$
    By trial and error search,
    you find that when $i = 0.03$,
    $FVIF = 4.5797$
    $i = 3\%$

Interest Factor Equation

$FVA = PMT(FVIFA_{i,n})$
$= \$200(FVIFA_{3\%,4})$
$= \$200(4.1836)$
$= \$836.72$

$PVA = PMT(PVIFA_{i,n})$
$\$20,000 = PMT(PVIFA_{1\%,60})$
$\$20,000 = PMT(44.9550)$
$PMT = \$444.89$

$FV = PV(FVIF_{i,n})$
$\$102 = \$2(FVIF_{i,30})$
$51 = FVIF_{i,30}$
Go to table in Appendix A.1
$FVIF_{14\%,30} = 50.950$
$i = 14\%$

$PVA = PMT(PVIFA_{i,n})$
$\$10,000 = \$2,183.55(PVIFA_{i,5})$
$4.5797 = PVIFA_{i,5}$
Go to table in Appendix A.4
$PVIFA_{3\%,5} = 4.5797$
$i = 3\%$

Chapter 4

5 RISK and RATE of RETURN

OVERVIEW

The objective of business financial management is to maximize shareholder wealth through maximization of stock price. Stock price depends on (1) the size of expected cash flows to shareholders, (2) the risk of the cash flows, and (3) the timing of the cash flows. Chapter 4 showed how the timing of cash flows affected their value. In this chapter, the concept of *risk* and its effect on stock price is explored. The chapter adopts the investor's viewpoint to explain (1) the definition of risk, (2) the measurement of risk, and (3) the relationship between risk and rate of return.

OUTLINE

Risk is the uncertainty surrounding the expected rate of return on an investment. Risk involves the possibility that the actual return will differ from the expected return.

- To reduce exposure to risk, many investors choose to invest in more than one security, which is called *diversification*. A holding of two or more securities is referred to as a *portfolio*.

To understand the concept of risk, one must first know how to calculate an expected rate of return. The expected return from investing in a stock is:

Chapter 5

$$\overline{K} = P_1 K_1 + P_2 K_2 + \ldots + P_n K_n$$

where $\overline{K}$ = expected rate of return, P = probability of a possible return occurring, K = possible rate of return, and n = number of possible rates of return. A listing of possible returns and their associated probabilities of occurrence is called a *probability distribution*. The expected return is the sum of the probabilities multiplied by the respective possibilities.

■ For example, suppose you are considering two stocks, Stock A and Stock B, which have the following probability distributions:

Stock A		Stock B	
P	K	P	K
0.25	0.30	0.25	0.06
0.45	0.15	0.45	0.12
0.30	0.05	0.30	0.18

The expected rate of return for Stock A is:

$$\overline{K}_A = (0.25)(0.30) + (0.45)(0.15) + (0.30)(0.05)$$
$$= 0.075 + 0.0675 + 0.015$$
$$= 0.1575$$

The expected rate of return for Stock B is:

$$\overline{K}_B = (0.25)(0.06) + (0.45)(0.12) + (0.30)(0.18)$$
$$= 0.015 + 0.054 + 0.054$$
$$= 0.123$$

The expected portfolio return is a weighted average of the expected returns of the individual stocks in the portfolio:

$$\text{Expected portfolio return} = W_1 \overline{K}_1 + W_2 \overline{K}_2 + \ldots + W_n \overline{K}_n$$

where W = weight reflecting an individual stock's value as a percentage of the total portfolio value, and $\overline{K}$ = expected rate of return for each individual stock in the portfolio.

- For example, suppose you bought 200 shares of Stock A at $10 per share and 200 shares of Stock B at $15 per share. To calculate the expected portfolio return, you must first calculate the weights reflecting each stock's value as a percentage of the total portfolio value:

$$\text{Total portfolio value} = (200)(\$10) + (200)(\$15)$$
$$= \$2,000 + \$3,000$$
$$= \$5,000$$

$$W_A = \$2,000/\$5,000 = 0.40$$
$$W_B = \$3,000/\$5,000 = 0.60$$

$$\text{Expected portfolio return} = (0.40)(0.1575) + (0.60)(0.123)$$
$$= 0.0630 + 0.0738$$
$$= 0.1368$$

Once an expected return has been determined, a standard deviation can be calculated as a measure of total risk. Standard deviation measures the variability of possible returns in a probability distribution and is calculated using the following steps:

(1) Calculate the deviation of each possible return from the expected return:

$$(K - \overline{K})$$

(2) Square each deviation:

$$(K - \overline{K})^2$$

(3) Multiply each squared deviation by the probability of its occurrence:

$$P(K - \overline{K})^2$$

(4) Sum the products from Step 3 to obtain the *variance* of returns:

$$\sigma^2 = \Sigma P(K - \overline{K})^2$$

Chapter 5

(5) Take the square root of the variance to obtain the standard deviation:

$$\sigma = \sqrt{\sigma^2}$$

■ For Stock A above, the standard deviation is:

$$\sigma_A = \sqrt{0.25(0.30-0.1575)^2 + 0.45(0.15-0.1575)^2 + 0.30(0.05-0.1575)^2}$$
$$= \sqrt{0.005077 + 0.000025 + 0.003467}$$
$$= \sqrt{0.008569} = 0.0926$$

For Stock B above, the standard deviation is:

$$\sigma_B = \sqrt{0.25(0.06-0.123)^2 + 0.45(0.12-0.123)^2 + 0.30(0.18-0.123)^2}$$
$$= \sqrt{0.000992 + 0.000004 + 0.000975}$$
$$= \sqrt{0.001971} = 0.0444$$

The larger the standard deviation, the greater the chance that an actual return will vary from an expected value, indicating greater risk. Smaller standard deviations indicate less variability and lower risk.

■ In the example of Stock A and Stock B, Stock A has a standard deviation of 0.0926, which is larger than Stock B's standard deviation of 0.0444. Thus, Stock A has greater risk than Stock B. There is a greater chance that Stock A's actual return will vary from its expected return of 0.1575 than there is that Stock B's actual return will vary from its expected return of 0.123.

■ A standard deviation of zero indicates that no risk is present; that is, there is no chance that the actual return will vary from the expected return.

When analysts cannot identify possible returns and probabilities, they often use a sample of past returns to calculate an estimated standard deviation.

Chapter 5

- An expected return (K_{avg}) is calculated by taking the mathematical average of the past returns(K_t). The estimated standard deviation is then calculated as:

$$\text{Estimated } \sigma = \sqrt{\Sigma(K_t - K_{avg})^2/(n-1)}$$

- For example, suppose ABC Corporation had rates of return for the past three years of 0.10, 0.25, and -0.05. The expected return is:

$$K_{avg} = (0.10 + 0.25 - 0.05)/3 = 0.10$$

The estimated standard deviation is:

$$\text{Estimated } \sigma = \sqrt{[(0.10-0.10)^2 + (0.25-0.10)^2 + (-0.05-0.10)^2]/(3-1)}$$

$$= \sqrt{0.045/2}$$

$$= 0.15$$

- While the estimated σ is a satisfactory measure of future variability, K_{avg} is not a good indicator of expected future return because rates of return on individual stocks tend to vary too much year to year.

Theoretically, risk in a two-stock portfolio can be totally eliminated if the returns of the two stocks always move in the opposite direction of each other. In reality, stock returns tend to change in the same direction. The way that returns move together is known as correlation.

- When stock returns move in the same direction, they are *positively correlated*. When they move in the same direction by the exact same magnitude, they are *perfectly positively correlated*.

- Stock returns are *negatively correlated* when they move in opposite directions, and are *perfectly negatively correlated* when they move in the opposite direction by the same degree.

- Zero correlation indicates that returns do not move together in any systematic way.

Chapter 5

Information about one series provides no information about the other.

■ A portfolio composed of stocks with perfect negative correlation eliminates risk completely. On the other hand, a portfolio of stocks with perfect positive correlation does not reduce risk at all. The risk is the same as if the investor put all of his or her money in just one stock.

Most stocks tend to be positively correlated, but not perfectly so. The lack of perfect positive correlation enables investors to reduce risk through diversification.

■ Combining different stocks into a portfolio reduces total risk as measured by the standard deviation.

Total risk is the sum of diversifiable risk and nondiversifiable risk.

■ Diversifiable risk, also known as *unsystematic risk* or *company-specific risk*, arises from unexpected events that affect only one company. These unexpected events, like a fire, lawsuit, or death of a key corporate officer, cause returns and stock prices to change in ways investors cannot anticipate.

Exposure to diversifiable risk can be virtually eliminated by holding a well-diversified portfolio.

■ As the number of stocks in a portfolio increases, diversifiable risk approaches zero. On average, a portfolio consisting of approximately twenty randomly selected stocks with equal dollar investments would eliminate most of the diversifiable risk.

■ As diversifiable risk decreases, total risk decreases as well. Because diversifiable risk constitutes about 50 percent of the total risk of a typical common stock, eliminating it through diversification is clearly beneficial. Studies of historical returns show that the standard deviation of a typical stock is about 30 percent; the standard deviation of a portfolio of all stocks is only about 15 percent.

Nondiversifiable risk arises from unexpected changes in general economic conditions that affect all stocks simultaneously. Investors cannot reduce nondiversifiable risk simply by diversifying.

■ Nondiversifiable risk is also known as *systematic risk* or *market risk*. Since investors eliminate exposure to diversifiable risk by investing in a well-diversified portfolio, nondiversifiable risk becomes the only relevant part of total risk.

The standard deviation reflects both diversifiable and nondiversifiable risk. Because risk-averse investors hold well-diversified portfolios that eliminate diversifiable risk, another measure of risk that reflects just the *nondiversifiable* portion is needed. Beta (ß) has been developed as a measure of nondiversifiable risk.

■ Beta is a regression coefficient that provides an estimate of how a particular stock's historical rates of return relate to returns on a market index. *By definition, a beta value of 1.0 indicates that a stock has nondiversifiable risk equal to that of the market portfolio of all stocks.* Percentage changes in the price of the stock tend to be the same as those of the market index. The stock is said to have *average* risk.

■ Betas greater than 1.0 indicate nondiversifiable risk greater than that of the market and are considered *above-average risk*. Betas below 1.0 indicate less market risk and are considered *below-average risk*. Most betas fall within the range of 0.70 to 1.60.

A portfolio beta is the weighted average of the stock betas in the portfolio and can be calculated as follows:

$$\beta_p = W_1\beta_1 + W_2\beta_2 + ... + W_n\beta_n$$

Weights are assigned reflecting each stock's dollar value as a percentage of portfolio dollar value.

■ For example, suppose you purchase 100 shares of Stock X at $15 per share, 100 shares of Stock Y at $25 per share, and 100 shares of Stock Z at $30 per share. The betas of these stocks are as follows:

Stock	Beta
X	0.90
Y	1.15
Z	1.40

To calculate the portfolio beta, the total value of the portfolio and the individual stock

Chapter 5

weights must first be determined:

$$\text{Total portfolio value} = (100)(\$15) + (100)(\$25) + (100)(\$30)$$
$$= \$1,500 + \$2,500 + \$3,000$$
$$= \$7,000$$

$$W_X = \$1,500/\$7,000 = 0.21$$
$$W_Y = \$2,500/\$7,000 = 0.36$$
$$W_Z = \$3,000/\$7,000 = 0.43$$

$$\beta_p = (0.21)(0.90) + (0.36)(1.15) + (0.43)(1.40)$$
$$= 0.189 + 0.414 + 0.602$$
$$= 1.205$$

- The beta of a stock measures its contribution to the riskiness of a portfolio. Adding high-beta stocks to a portfolio increases its risk, while adding low-beta stocks lowers its risk.

The capital asset pricing model (CAPM) relates a stock's beta to its required rate of return. Required rate of return is the rate of return investors require to compensate for exposure to nondiversifiable risk. Risk-averse investors require higher rates of return on stocks with larger betas.

- The required rate of return is equal to (1) the *risk-free rate of return* (R_f) plus (2) a *risk premium* that consists of the market price of risk adjusted to reflect the nondiversifiable risk of a particular stock.

The CAPM calculates required rate of return as:

$$K_c = R_f + (K_m - R_f)\beta$$

where K_c = the required rate of return on a common stock; R_f = risk-free rate of return; K_m = required rate of return on the market portfolio; and β = level of nondiversifiable risk for a particular stock.

- Values for R_f and K_m are the *same* for *all* companies. Each stock's beta is what differentiates its required rate of return, making it higher for betas above 1.0 and lower for betas below 1.0. A stock with a beta of 1.0 would have the same required return as the market portfolio, K_m, since it has the same risk as the market.

■ For example, Stock P has a beta of 1.35 and Stock Q has a beta of 0.85. If the risk-free rate of return is 8 percent and the required return on the market is 12 percent, the required rates of return on Stock P and Stock Q are:

$$\text{Stock P: } K_c = 0.08 + (0.12-0.08)(1.35)$$
$$= 0.08 + 0.054$$
$$= 0.134$$

$$\text{Stock Q: } K_c = 0.08 + (0.12-0.08)(0.85)$$
$$= 0.08 + 0.034$$
$$= 0.114$$

Stock P has above-average risk ($\beta=1.35$), and its investors require a return greater than the market return as compensation. Stock Q, with below-average risk ($\beta=0.85$), has a required return lower than the market required rate of return.

The CAPM can also be portrayed graphically. The security market line (SML) shows the trade-off between nondiversifiable risk and the rate of return investors require on common stock.

■ The SML can be constructed with two points: (1) when beta = zero, $K_c = R_f$, so the first point is $(0, R_f)$; (2) when beta = 1.0, $K_c = K_m$, making the second point $(1.0, K_m)$.

■ The slope of the SML is $(K_m - R_f)$, the market price of risk. This is the return in excess of the risk-free rate necessary to induce investors to buy an average stock with the same risk as the market portfolio. Changes in slope reflect changes in risk-aversion in the marketplace.

Note that the SML reflects marketwide conditions, based on R_f and K_m. It should not be constructed using the beta and required return for a particular stock or portfolio.

Equilibrium occurs when the *expected* rate of return on a stock is equal to its *required* rate of return, and the stock price is equal to its intrinsic value. When the

Chapter 5

beta and required return of a stock in equilibrium are plotted on a graph, the point falls *on* the SML.

- The intrinsic value of an asset is based on the present value of its expected future cash flows. Intrinsic value can be calculated using the perpetuity model and incorporates the required rate of return:

    Intrinsic value = Expected cash flow/Required rate of return

- Expected rate of return can be calculated as:

    Expected rate of return = Expected cash flow/Stock price

If the expected return exceeds the required return, the market price of the stock will be lower than its intrinsic value, and the stock will be considered *underpriced*. Graphically, it would fall on a point above the SML.

- Under this condition, investors would eagerly buy this stock. As investors bid for the stock, they bid up the price and bid down the expected return, thereby restoring equilibrium.

When the expected return is less than the required return, the market price of the stock will be higher than its intrinsic value, and investors will consider the stock *overpriced*. When plotted, this stock would fall below the SML.

- In this case, investors would want to sell the stock. The increase in supply of the stock would make its market price drop, thereby raising the expected return, until equilibrium is restored.

The CAPM can be used to judge whether a stock price is too high or too low, based on its expected return relative to its required return.

- A stock's required rate of return is calculated using the model, and investors buy or sell the stock based on the difference between expected and required return, causing the stock price to move into equilibrium.

Inflation causes investors to require higher rates of return.

- Inflation is a rise in the average price of goods and services that causes a decline in the purchasing power of money. Expected inflation is incorporated into the risk-free rate of return (R_f) as follows:

    R_f = Real rate of return + Premium for expected inflation

    Changes in the expected inflation rate affect the risk-free rate, and consequently, all required rates of return. An increase in expected inflation results in an upward, parallel shift of the SML. Required rates of return are higher for all levels of beta.

- *Note that changes in inflation do not change the slope of the SML -- changes in risk-aversion do.* Since the risk premium reflecting risk aversion remains constant, both R_f *and* K_m must increase by equal amounts when expected inflation increases. Beta is unaffected by changes in expected inflation.

There are difficulties in applying the capital asset pricing model.

- These include: (1) estimating a reliable beta for the future based on historical data; (2) deciding whether to use the yield on short- or long-term U.S. Treasury bonds as the proxy for the risk-free rate; (3) estimating the market price of risk ($K_m - R_f$); and (4) using beta alone as the measure of risk, because not all investors diversify their investments.

Financial managers need to understand the impact of investors' perceived risk on required rate of return and stock price.

- Any managerial decision that makes a company's stock returns more sensitive to broad changes in stock market prices causes an increase in the stock's beta. Any decision that makes the returns less sensitive decreases beta. A company's *investment* and *financing* decisions potentially affect beta, and, therefore, required rate of return.

- When the expected rate of return differs from the required rate of return, intrinsic value differs from the stock price. The buying and selling by investors will drive the market price to the intrinsic value, where expected and required rates of return are equal, and the stock price is in equilibrium.

Chapter 5

GLOSSARY OF KEY TERMS

beta, ß: measure of nondiversifiable risk

capital asset pricing model (CAPM): model that relates required rate of return to the risk-free rate plus a risk premium

correlation: degree to which a series of returns changes systematically with another series

diversifiable risk: portion of stock risk that is unique to the company; also called unsystematic risk or company-specific risk

diversification: investing in more than one security to reduce risk

expected portfolio return: weighted average of the expected returns on the stocks in a portfolio

fixed costs: operating costs that do not change as output changes

intrinsic value: value of an asset based on the present value of its expected future cash flows

market portfolio: portfolio of all risky securities; Standard & Poor's 500 Index is often used as a proxy for the market portfolio

market price of risk, $(k_m - R_f)$: required rate of return on the market portfolio (or average-risk stock) less the risk-free rate; in the CAPM, the slope of the security market line

nondiversifiable risk: portion of stock risk that arises from general economic conditions affecting all firms simultaneously; also called systematic risk or market risk

portfolio beta, $ß_p$: weighted average of the stock betas in a portfolio

probability distribution: listing of possible returns and their associated probabilities of occurrence

risk premium, $(K_m - R_f)ß$: additional percentage points required by investors for investing in risky securities; in the CAPM, the excess return over the risk-free rate

risk-free rate of return, R_f: rate of return known with certainty; estimated with yields on U.S. Treasury securities

standard deviation, σ: measure of dispersion around the expected return of a distribution of possible returns; a measure of total risk

variable costs: operating costs that change as output changes

variance, σ^2: the square of standard deviation

Chapter 5

MULTIPLE CHOICE SELF-TEST

1. Risk-averse investors

    a. shouldn't invest in the stock market
    b. shouldn't invest in corporate bonds
    c. should only purchase U.S. Treasury securities
    d. should keep their money under their mattresses
    e. require higher rates of return on higher-risk investments

2. Standard deviation is the appropriate measure of

    a. diversifiable risk
    b. nondiversifiable risk
    c. market risk
    d. company-specific risk
    e. total risk

3. The degree to which a series of returns changes systematically with another series is called

    a. systematic risk
    b. standard deviation
    c. correlation
    d. diversification
    e. capital asset pricing model

4. The total risk of a portfolio containing two stocks with perfectly positively correlated returns

    a. can be lower than the risk of the lower-risk stock
    b. cannot be lower than the risk of the lower-risk stock
    c. depends on the expected value of the lower-risk stock
    d. depends on the expected value of the higher-risk stock
    e. is always equal to 1.0

77

Chapter 5

5. For successful diversification, an investor should

   a. combine stocks that are less than perfectly positively correlated
   b. hold at least 100 different stocks
   c. combine only stock with correlation coefficients equal to zero
   d. always hold risk-free assets
   e. sell stocks and buy bonds

6. Which of the following unexpected events is an example of diversifiable risk?

   a. federal tax rate changes
   b. recession
   c. inflation increases
   d. changes in the general level of interest rates
   e. none of the above

7. The beta coefficient of the market portfolio

   a. varies over time
   b. is between -1.0 and zero
   c. can be between zero and +1.0
   d. is equal to +1.0
   e. is undefined

8. According to the capital asset pricing model, the marketplace rewards investors with a percentage premium for incurring

   a. market risk
   b. company-specific risk
   c. diversifiable risk
   d. unsystematic risk
   e. none of the above

Chapter 5

9. Which of the following is used as a proxy for the risk-free rate of return?

    a. U.S. Treasury bond rate
    b. return on corporate bonds
    c. return on commercial paper
    d. interest rate on passbook savings accounts
    e. return on the market index

10. When the expected rate of return on a stock exceeds the required rate, investors will

    a. buy the stock because it is overpriced
    b. buy the stock because it is underpriced
    c. sell the stock because it is overpriced
    d. sell the stock because it is underpriced
    e. sell the stock because it is too risky

11. A decline in the purchasing power of money as measured by an increase in the average price level of goods and services is called

    a. diversification
    b. arbitrage pricing
    c. inflation
    d. unsystematic risk
    e. none of the above

12. If investors expect an increase in the rate of inflation, the security market line will

    a. move up by the amount of the expected change
    b. move down by the amount of the expected change
    c. have a steeper slope
    d. have a flatter slope
    e. remain unchanged

Chapter 5

PROBLEMS

Use the following information for Problems 1 and 2:

The rate of return on the stock of Oklahoma Oil Company is dependent on events in the Middle East.

Status of Middle East	Probability of Occurrence	Rate of Return
serious trouble	0.50	20%
limited trouble	0.25	10%
calm	0.25	6%

1. What is the expected rate of return on Oklahoma Oil Company stock?

2. What is the standard deviation of the rate of return on Oklahoma Oil Company stock?

3. Calculate the expected portfolio return, assuming that you purchased 100 shares of Stock A, 150 shares of Stock B, and 200 shares of Stock C.

Stock	Expected Return	Price Per Share
A	12%	$32.00
B	5%	$ 8.50
C	20%	$25.00

4. Suppose you invest equal amounts into Stocks Y and Z, which have the following probability distributions:

Stock Y		Stock Z	
P	K	P	K
0.30	0.04	0.30	0.02
0.60	0.08	0.60	0.10
0.10	0.16	0.10	0.24

Calculate the portfolio standard deviation.

Chapter 5

5. The beta of Ace's stock is 1.8. The beta of Deuce's stock is 1.4. Each trades for $10.00 per share. If you hold 200 shares of Ace and 300 shares of Deuce, what is your portfolio beta?

6. The Shore Sand Company has a beta of 1.8. If the risk-free rate is 6 percent and the required return on the market portfolio is 11 percent, what is the required rate of return on Shore Sand's stock?

Use the following information for Problems 8 and 9:

An investor has decided to purchase 100 shares of each of the following stocks:

Stock	Beta	Price Per Share
X	0.90	$20
Y	1.10	$30
Z	1.30	$50

The risk-free rate of return is 7 percent and the required return on the market is 10 percent.

7. What is the portfolio beta?

8. What is the required rate of return on the portfolio?

9. Stock Q is expected to generate an 18 percent rate of return. If the risk-free rate of return is 9 percent, the required return on the market is 15 percent, and Stock Q's beta is 1.6, will investors want to buy stock Q?

10. Stock J has a beta of 0.95 and a required return of 11.8 percent. The market price of risk is 4 percent. If inflation decreases by 2 percentage points, what will be the new risk-free rate of return?

Chapter 5

SOLUTIONS TO MULTIPLE CHOICE SELF-TEST

1. e   7. d
2. e   8. a
3. c   9. a
4. b   10. b
5. a   11. c
6. e   12. a

SOLUTIONS TO PROBLEMS

1. $\bar{K}$ = (0.50)(0.20) + (0.25)(0.10) + (0.25)(0.06)
   = 0.10 + 0.025 + 0.015
   = 0.14, or 14%

2. σ^2 = (0.20-0.14)^2(0.50) + (0.10-0.14)^2(0.25)
      + (0.06-0.14)^2(0.25)
   = 0.0018 + 0.0004 + 0.0016
   = 0.0038
   σ = 0.0616, or 6.16%

3. Total Investment = (100)($32.00) + (150)($8.50)
                    + (200)($25.00)
                   = $3,200 + $1,275 + $5,000
                   = $9,475

Chapter 5

Weight$_A$ = $3,200/$9,475 = .34
Weight$_B$ = $1,275/$9,475 = .13
Weight$_C$ = $5,000/$9,475 = .53

Expected
Portfolio   = (0.34)(0.12) + (0.13)(0.05) + (0.53)(0.20)
Return
            = 0.0408 + 0.0065 + 0.1060
            = 0.1533, or 15.33%

4. Portfolio Probability Distribution:

P	K
0.30	(0.50)(0.04)+(0.50)(0.02) = 0.03
0.60	(0.50)(0.08)+(0.50)(0.10) = 0.09
0.10	(0.50)(0.16)+(0.50)(0.24) = 0.20

Expected
Portfolio   = (0.30)(0.03) + (0.60)(0.09) + (0.10)(0.20)
Return
            = 0.009 + 0.054 + 0.020
            = 0.083, or 8.3%

Portfolio Variance = $(0.03-0.083)^2(0.30)$
                     + $(0.09-0.083)^2(0.60)$
                     + $(0.20-0.083)^2(0.10)$
                   =   0.0008427 + 0.0000294 + 0.0013689
                   =   0.002241

Portfolio Standard Deviation = $\sqrt{0.002241}$
                             = 0.0473, or 4.73%

Chapter 5

5. Total Investment = (200)($10) + (300)($10)
    $$= \$200 + \$300$$
    $$= \$500$$

    Weight for Ace   = $200/$500 = 0.40
    Weight for Deuce = $300/$500 = 0.60

    Portfolio Beta = (0.40)(1.8) + (0.60)(1.4)
    $$= 0.72 + 0.84$$
    $$= 1.56$$

6. K_c = 6% + (11%-6%)(1.8)
    $$= 6\% + 9\%$$
    $$= 15\%$$

7. Total Investment = (100)($20) + (100)($30) + (100)($50)
    $$= \$2,000 + \$3,000 + \$5,000$$
    $$= \$10,000$$

    $Weight_X$ = $2,000/$10,000 = 0.20
    $Weight_Y$ = $3,000/$10,000 = 0.30
    $Weight_Z$ = $5,000/$10,000 = 0.50

    Portfolio Beta = (0.20)(0.90)+(0.30)(1.10)+(0.50)(1.30)
    $$= 0.18 + 0.33 + 0.65$$
    $$= 1.16$$

8. K_c = 7% + (10%-7%)(1.16)
    $$= 7\% + 3.48\%$$
    $$= 10.48\%$$

9. K_c = 9% + (15%-9%)(1.6)
    $$= 9\% + 9.6\%$$
    $$= 18.6\%$$

    Since required exceeds expected, investors will try to sell Stock Q.

10. Solve for original R_f:
    $$11.8\% = R_f + (4\%)(0.95)$$
    $$11.8\% = R_f + 3.8\%$$
    $$R_f = 8\%$$

    After decrease in inflation: $R_f = 8\% - 2\% = 6\%$

Chapter 5

6 SECURITY VALUATION

OVERVIEW

The *intrinsic value* of a security is the present value of its expected cash flows. In the this chapter the view of an investor is taken to estimate the intrinsic value of bonds, preferred stock, and common stock. This process is called *valuation*. An understanding of how investors value these securities will provide the basis for determining investors required rate of return and calculating a company's *cost of capital* in Chapter 7.

OUTLINE

The intrinsic value of a security is determined by (1) expected cash flows from the security (e.g., interest income from bonds or dividends from stock) and (2) the rate of return required by investors as compensation for their opportunity cost. The required rate of return is used as the discount rate in calculating the present value of the expected cash flows.

- Each investor may come up with a different intrinsic value for a security because each may estimate different future cash flows and require a different rate of return. It is the *consensus* judgment of investors that gives rise to *market value*, the price at which a security trades.

Chapter 6

Professional investors compare market value with intrinsic value to decide whether they want to buy or sell a security.

- If intrinsic value exceeds market value, investors will buy the security (or not sell those they already own).

- If market value exceeds intrinsic value, investors will sell securities they own (or not buy any).

- If intrinsic value equals market value, the security is in *equilibrium*, a condition in which the price reflects all relevant information and there is no tendency for the price to change.

An efficient capital market is one in which security prices quickly reflect new information regarding the amount or timing of expected cash flows, causing price to equal intrinsic value. The assertion that security prices reflect all known information is called the *efficient market hypothesis (EMH)*.

- The *weak* form of the EMH asserts that the current price of a security reflects all information contained in *past* prices and rates of return.

- The *semi-strong* form of the EMH asserts that the current price of a security reflects *all publicly available* information.

- The *strong* form of the EMH asserts that the current price of a security reflects *all* information, public *and* private.

- Empirical evidence supports the *weak* and *semi-strong* forms of the EMH. Investors cannot consistently pick under- and overpriced stocks to earn abnormal returns using publicly available information. The release of new information about a security leads to an almost immediate change in its stock price, making it difficult for investors to "beat the market."

- The *strong* form of the EMH postulates that stock prices reflect not only all publicly available information but *insider* information as well. This form has been proven to be false, since individuals *have* made abnormal returns trading on insider information. Of course, such trading was made illegal under the Securities Exchange Act of 1934.

Chapter 6

The intrinsic value of a bond is the present value of its expected cash flows. Investors receive two forms of cash flows from owning bonds: (1) fixed interest payments at regular intervals and (2) the repayment of principal when the bond matures.

- The interest payments on a bond are based on its *coupon rate*. Annual interest equals the coupon rate times the principal of the bond. Since most bonds pay interest every six months, the annual interest payment must be divided in half to determine the correct semiannual payment. The interest payments are an annuity since they are fixed in amount and are paid at regular intervals.

- Bond principal is called *par value*, or *face value*, and is usually $1,000 per bond. Investors are paid the par value when the bond matures.

To find the intrinsic value of a bond, the present value of the interest payments are added to the present value of the principal. The discount rate to use is the current market rate of interest, or the investor's required rate of return -- *not* the coupon rate.

- In valuing both the interest payments *and* the principal, semiannual compounding and semiannual time periods must be used if the bond pays semiannual interest. K_d, the annual market rate of interest, must be divided by 2, and *n* must be adjusted to reflect the remaining number of semiannual compounding periods until the bond matures.

- To calculate the present value of the interest payments, the mathematical equation for the present value of an annuity, the interest factor equation for the present value of an annuity, or a financial calculator may be used.

- Since the repayment of principal is a single cash flow, its present value must be calculated using the mathematical or interest factor equation for a single cash flow, or again, a financial calculator may be used.

- For example, suppose the coupon rate on a $1,000 bond is 8 percent, there are 15 years left until maturity, and the current market rate of interest is 6 percent. If interest is paid semiannually, the intrinsic value (VB) would be calculated as follows:

    Semiannual interest payments = (0.08 × $1,000)/2 = $80/2 = $40

Chapter 6

$$\text{Discount rate, } K_d = 0.06/2 = 0.03$$

Semiannual time periods, n = 15 years × 2 periods/year = 30 periods

$$\begin{aligned}
VB &= (\$40)[1-(1.03)^{-30}]/0.03 + (\$1{,}000)(1.03)^{-30} \\
&= (\$40)(19.6004) + (\$1{,}000)(0.4120) \\
&= \$784.02 + \$412.00 \\
&= \$1{,}196.02
\end{aligned}$$

In an efficient market, the intrinsic value and market price of the bond will both equal $1,196.02.

When the coupon rate on a bond exceeds the current market interest rate, the bond's price will be greater than its par value. The bond is said to be trading *at a premium*.

- In the example above, the coupon rate was 8 percent and the market rate was 6 percent. By paying $1,196.02 for the bond, an investor will earn a 6 percent annual rate of return compounded semiannually.

When the current market rate of interest exceeds the coupon rate, the bond will sell for less than its par value. The bond is said to be trading *at a discount*.

- Suppose that in the above example, the market rate had been 10 percent instead of 6 percent. The price of the bond would then be $846.30. By paying $846.30 for a bond with a coupon rate of 8 percent, the investor will earn a 10 percent annual rate of return compounded semiannually.

When the coupon rate equals the market rate, the bond will sell for its par value.

- Issuers and their investment bankers try to set the coupon rate to equal the current market rate when the bonds are first issued so that the bonds sell for par value. However, sometimes the issue price of the bond must be adjusted upwards or downwards from par to attract investors. If the bonds are underpriced, the issuing company or the investment bankers stand to lose some of their proceeds or gross profit. If the bonds are overpriced, investors will not want to purchase them and the issuing company and the investment bankers will have to lower the price to sell the bonds.

There is an inverse relationship between market interest rates and bond prices.

- In Chapter 4, the inverse relationship between discount rates and present value was introduced -- the higher the discount rate, the lower the present value, and conversely, the lower the discount rate, the higher the present value.

- With bonds, as market interest rates rise, the value (price) of the bond falls; and as market interest rates fall, the value (price) of the bond rises.

The potential difference between actual rates of return and expected rates of return, caused by unexpected changes in market interest rates, is called *interest rate risk*.

- All securities, including default-free U.S. Treasury securities, are subject to varying amounts of interest-rate risk. Other things being equal, the longer the maturity of a bond, the greater the interest rate risk will be.

The expected cash flow from owning a share of preferred stock is a stated, level dividend that is paid indefinitely. Therefore, finding the intrinsic value of preferred stock involves finding the present value of a perpetuity.

- Dividends on preferred stock are stated (1) as a percent of the par value of the stock or (2) as a dollar amount.

- The equation for the intrinsic value of preferred stock (VP) is:

$$VP = D_p/K_p$$

where D_p equals the annual dividend and K_p equals the investor's annual required rate of return.

- For example, suppose a preferred stock has a $100 par value and pays a dividend of 10 percent. If investors require a 12 percent rate of return, the intrinsic value would be:

$$VP = [(0.10)(\$100)]/0.12 = \$10/0.12 = \$83.33$$

Chapter 6

- Some preferred stock is *callable*, meaning that the issuers can redeem the shares by paying stockholders a prespecified call price. To calculate the intrinsic value of callable preferred stock, the present value of the dividends expected prior to the call are added to the present value of the call price.

Estimating the intrinsic value of common stock is more difficult than doing so for bonds and preferred stock because the expected cash flows from owning common stock vary over time, while cash flows from bonds and preferred stock are fixed.

- Common shareholders may receive cash flows in the form of (1) cash dividends and (2) proceeds from the sale of the stock. To determine the intrinsic value, the present values of both cash flows are calculated using the required rate of return on the common stock as the discount rate.

The equation for the intrinsic value of common stock (VC) is:

$$VC = \text{PV of dividends} + \text{PV of future sale price}$$

$$= \sum_{t=1}^{n} D_t(1+K_c)^{-t} + P_n(1+K_c)^{-t}$$

- For example, suppose the estimated dividends on a share of common stock over the next three years are $2.00, $2.60, and $3.00, respectively, and it is estimated that the stock can be sold at the end of three years for $35. If investors require a 20 percent rate of return, the intrinsic value of the stock would be:

$$VC = [\$2.00(1.2)^{-1} + \$2.60(1.2)^{-2} + \$3.00(1.2)^{-3}] + \$35(1.2)^{-3}$$

$$= \$5.21 + \$20.25$$

$$= \$25.46$$

- The selling price of a share of stock is determined by the present value of the future dividends that the purchaser expects to receive. Since the selling price depends on expected future dividends, the value of common stock can be viewed *strictly in terms of a dividend stream*, ignoring any consideration of a future selling price.

Chapter 6

One model for determining the intrinsic value of common stock (based on dividend stream only) is the constant-growth model, also known as the Gordon model. This model assumes that dividends grow perpetually at a constant annual rate. The intrinsic value of common stock (VC) is calculated as:

$$VC = D_1/(K_c - g)$$

where D_1 equals the cash dividend expected *one year from now*; K_c equals the annual required rate of return; and g equals the expected annual rate of growth in the stock's dividends.

■ For example, suppose a company recently paid a $2.00 per share dividend on its common stock. Dividends are expected to grow at an annual rate of 10 percent. If investors require a 15 percent rate of return, the intrinsic value (VC) would be calculated as follows:

First, D_1, the *next* expected dividend must be determined:

$D_1 = D_0(1 + g)$, where D_0 equals the last dividend paid

$D_1 = \$2.00(1 + 0.10) = \$2.20$

Now, VC can be calculated:

$VC = \$2.20/(0.15 - 0.10)$
$= \$2.20/0.05$
$= \$44.00$

Note that increases in D_1 and g and decreases in K_c lead to increases in stock value, the objective of business financial management.

■ The constant-growth model can accommodate zero-growth stocks, which pay a constant dividend, by letting g = 0.

Investors expect the dividends of some stocks to grow at varying (nonconstant) rates.

■ Calculating the intrinsic value for a stock experiencing nonconstant growth in

Chapter 6

dividends involves the use of different growth rates that reflect the variation in the dividends over time. The exact procedure for calculating intrinsic value under nonconstant growth varies from scenario to scenario.

GLOSSARY OF KEY TERMS

at a discount: trading at a price below par value; said of a discount bond
at a premium: trading at a price above par value; said of a premium bond
call price: price a company pays to investors for early redemption of bonds or preferred stock
constant-growth (Gordon) model: model that equates intrinsic value with the present value of dividends growing at a constant rate into the indefinite future
efficient capital market: market in which security prices quickly reflect new information, causing price to equal intrinsic value
interest rate risk: risk due to unexpected changes in market interest rates; uncertainty in bond prices
market value: price at which a security trades
nonconstant-growth model: model for valuing stocks whose dividends investors expect will grow at varying rates
valuation: process of estimating the value of an asset
zero-coupon bond: bond that does not pay coupon interest; issued at discount from par
zero-growth stock: stock whose dividends investors expect will remain constant into the indefinite future; $g = 0$ in the constant growth model

Chapter 6

REVIEW OF KEY FORMULAS

Valuation

Bonds: $VB = (I/2)[1-(1+k_d/2)^{-2n}]/(k_d/2) + (Par)(1+k_d/2)^{-2n}$

Preferred Stock: $VP = D_p/K_p$

Common Stock: $VC = D_1/(K_c - g)$

MULTIPLE CHOICE SELF-TEST

1. If the market value of a stock exceeds its intrinsic value

   a. investors who own the stock will not sell their shares
   b. potential investors in the stock will not buy it
   c. potential investors in the stock will buy it
   d. the stock is in equilibrium
   e. none of the above

2. In an efficient market,

   a. everyone earns the market rate of return on investments
   b. it is possible to consistently earn abnormal returns trading on publicly available information
   c. intrinsic value equals market price
   d. security prices change slowly when new information becomes available, giving all investors a chance to react
   e. decreases in expected cash flows lead to increases in price

Chapter 6

3. Extensive research in finance has documented the fact that the stock market is not

    a. sensitive to changes in economic conditions
    b. weak-form efficient
    c. semistrong-form efficient
    d. strong-form efficient
    e. regulated

4. The market value of a bond varies inversely with

    a. the coupon rate
    b. the discount rate
    c. the face value
    d. the term to maturity
    e. all of the above

5. If a bond is selling at a premium relative to its par value

    a. its coupon rate must be equal to its YTM
    b. its coupon rate must be equal to the market rate of interest
    c. its coupon rate must exceed the market rate of interest
    d. its coupon rate must be lower than the market rate of interest
    e. its coupon rate must be lower than its YTM

6. Which of the following bonds would experience the greatest price change if the market rate of interest increased from 8% to 12%? Assume the bonds all have the same coupon rate.

    a. a bond that matures in six months
    b. a one-year bond
    c. a ten-year bond
    d. a twenty-year bond
    e. the bonds would all experience the same percentage price change

7. Valuing preferred stock involves the use of the

   a. perpetuity model
   b. constant-growth model
   c. nonconstant-growth model
   d. CAPM model
   e. arbitrage pricing model

8. An increase in preferred stockholders' required rate of return would

   a. increase the price of the preferred stock
   b. increase the dividend on the preferred stock
   c. decrease the price of the preferred stock
   d. decrease the dividend on the preferred stock
   e. not affect the price of the preferred stock

PROBLEMS

1. Alpha's bonds have a 7.25 percent coupon, paid semiannually, which mature in 15 years and have a par value of $1,000. The market rate of interest on similar-risk bonds is 8 percent. Find the current market price of Alpha's bonds.

2. What is the coupon rate on a bond that pays interest semiannually, has a $1,000 par value, and has 5 years to maturity? The bond is priced at $1,038.59, and the market rate of interest is 10 percent.

3. What is the value of a share of preferred stock that pays a 9 percent annual dividend on a $50 par value if investors require a 12 percent rate of return? What happens to the price if the required return drops to 10 percent?

Chapter 6

4. You have been researching the stock of a company in which you wish to invest. Expected dividends per year for the next four years are $1.50, $1.75, $2.05, and $2.15, respectively. If you estimate that the stock could be sold for $25.00 at the end of the fourth year (immediately after receiving the dividend), what is the most you would pay for the stock today if your required rate of return is 12 percent?

5. Rane Corp. just paid its common stockholders a $2.40 per share dividend. Dividends have been growing at a rate of 10 percent and are expected to continue at that rate for the foreseeable future. If shareholders require a 14 percent rate of return, what is the price of Rane's stock?

6. Analysts predict that Krypton Steel Company's annual dividend for the coming year will be $4.80, and that the company should continue to enjoy a 10 percent growth rate. Krypton's stock is 50 percent more volatile than the market. If the required return on the market is 16 percent and the risk-free rate of return is 8 percent, what is the price of Krypton's stock?

SOLUTIONS TO MULTIPLE CHOICE SELF-TEST

1. b
2. c
3. d
4. b
5. c
6. d
7. a
8. c

Chapter 6

SOLUTIONS TO PROBLEMS

1. $I/2 = (0.0725 \times \$1{,}000)/2 = \$36.25$
   $K_d/2 = 0.08/2 = 0.04$
   $2n = (2)(15) = 30$

   $VB = (\$36.25)[1-(1.04)^{-30}]/0.04 + (\$1{,}000)(1.04)^{-30}$
   $= (\$36.25)(17.2920) + (\$1{,}000)(0.3083)$
   $= \$626.84 + \$308.30$
   $= \$935.14$

2. $K_d/2 = 0.10/2 = 0.05$
   $2n = (2)(5) = 10$

   $\$1{,}038.59 = (I/2)[1-(1.05)^{-10}]/0.05 + (\$1{,}000)(0.05)^{-10}$
   $\$1{,}038.59 = (I/2)(7.7217) + (\$1{,}000)(0.6139)$
   $\$1{,}038.59 = (I/2)(7.7217) + \$613.90$
   $\$424.69 = (I/2)(7.7217)$
   $I/2 = \$55$
   $I = \$110$
   $\$110/\$1{,}000 = 0.11$, or 11%

3. $V_p = D_p/K_p$

   $D_p = (0.09)(\$50) = \$4.50$

   $V_p = \$4.50/0.12 = \$37.50$

   If $K_p = 10\%$, $V_p = \$4.50/0.10 = \$45.00$

   As K_p declines, VP increases

4. $VC = (\$1.50)(1.12)^{-1} + (\$1.75)(1.12)^{-2}$
   $+ (\$2.05)(1.12)^{-3} + (\$2.15)(1.12)^{-4}$
   $+ (\$25.00)(1.12)^{-4}$

Chapter 6

$$= (\$1.50)(0.8929) + (\$1.75)(0.7972) + (\$2.05)(0.7118)$$
$$+ (\$2.15)(0.6355) + (\$25.00)(0.6355)$$

$$= \$1.34 + \$1.40 + \$1.46 + \$1.37 + \$15.89$$
$$= \$21.46$$

5. $VC = D_1/(K_c - g)$

   $D_1 = D_0(1 + g)$
   $= \$2.40(1 + 0.10)$
   $= \$2.64$

   $VC = \$2.64/(0.14 - 0.10)$
   $= \$66.00$

6. $VC = D_1/(K_c - g)$

   $K_c = R_f + (K_m - R_f)\beta$
   $= 0.08 + (0.16 - 0.08)(1.5)$
   $= 0.20$

   $VC = \$4.80/(0.20 - 0.10)$
   $= \$48.00$

7 COST of CAPITAL

OVERVIEW

In this chapter, the different sources of financing used by the firm are discussed and the valuation models introduced in Chapter 6 are used to estimate the component costs of capital. The components costs of capital are then combined to form a weighted-average cost of capital for a company. By looking at the impact of the firm's *financing* decisions (debt-equity mix) on its average cost of capital, the financial manager should be able, in theory, to construct a capital structure that minimizes the average cost of capital and maximizes shareholder wealth. The chapter concludes with an examination of the *marginal* cost of capital and its role in selecting capital projects for *investment* decisions.

OUTLINE

The sources of capital to a company are: (1) corporate bonds, (2) preferred stock, and (3) common stock. The *component cost of capital* depends on the rate of return required by the providers of the capital -- bondholders, preferred stockholders, and common shareholders. It is the percentage cost of each source of capital that must be paid to compensate investors for their opportunity cost.

- The price of a security is combined with an estimate of its expected cash flows in a present-value equation to solve for the required rate of return. Adjustments may be necessary to account for tax effects and flotation costs.

Chapter 7

The cost of capital and the value of a company are inversely related.

■ The combined market values of a company's bonds, preferred stock, and common stock equal the company's total market value. If the cost of a company's capital can be reduced, or the price of its securities increased, the company's market value will be increased.

The percentage cost of bonds issued by a company is the rate of return required by investors in the bonds, adjusted for flotation costs and tax effects.

■ For income tax purposes, the interest paid on bonds is deductible as an expense. Consequently, the cost of bonds is reduced by the savings in taxes. If K_i is the after-tax percentage cost, K_d is the required rate of return, and T is the company's marginal tax rate, the relationship is:

$$K_i = K_d(1 - T)$$

The required rate of return on a bond, K_d, is also called the *yield to maturity (YTM)*. The YTM is the discount rate that makes a bond's price equal to the present value of its future cash flows (interest and repayment of principal).

■ When companies issue bonds at par value, the YTM equals the coupon rate.

■ When bonds are selling at a price other than par, the YTM can be found using an iterative procedure in which calculations are repeated using different discount rates until one is found that equates the present value of the cash flows to the bond price.

■ For example, suppose that a bond with a market price of $771 and a par value of $1,000 matures in 10 years. The coupon rate on the bond is 8 percent and interest is paid semiannually. Calculation of the YTM involves the following:

Semiannual interest payments = (0.08 × $1,000)/2, or $40.

There are 20 semiannual interest payments remaining until maturity (10 years × 2 periods/year).

$$\$771 = (\$40) \times [1-(1+k_d/2)^{-20}]/(k_d/2) + (\$1,000) \times (1+k_d/2)^{-20}$$

Chapter 7

Through trial and error, one finds that 6 percent is the discount rate that makes the present value of the future cash flows equal to $771:

$$\$771 = (\$40)(11.4699) + (\$1,000)(0.3118)$$
$$\$771 = \$771$$

The semiannual rate must be doubled to reflect the annual YTM. In this example, the YTM is 12 percent per year (6% × 2).

Once the YTM has been determined, it must be adjusted to reflect tax effects. Remember that YTM equals K_d, the required rate of return on bonds.

- In the example above, if the firm's marginal tax rate is 40 percent, the after-tax percentage cost of bonds is:

$$K_i = K_d(1 - T)$$

$$K_i = (0.12)(1 - .40) = 0.072, \text{ or } 7.2\%$$

The yield to maturity can be approximated by dividing the average annual dollar return on the bond by the average annual investment in the bond.

$$\text{Approximate YTM} = \{I + [(\text{Par} - \text{VB})/n]\}/[(\text{VB} + \text{Par})/2]$$

$$I = \text{annual interest}; n = \text{years to maturity}$$

- Following the previous example, an approximate YTM would be calculated as:

$$\text{Approximate YTM} = \{\$80 + [(\$1,000 - \$771)/10]\}/[(\$771 + \$1,000)/2]$$
$$= \$102.90/\$885.50$$
$$= 0.116, \text{ or } 11.6\%, \text{ close to the exact YTM of } 12\%$$

The flotation costs of issuing new bonds in the primary, capital market should also be considered in calculating the percentage cost of bonds.

Chapter 7

- The payment of investment banking fees, accounting and legal expenses, printing costs, and other expenses relating to the issuance of new bonds reduces the proceeds to the issuing company and increases the cost of capital to the firm.

- To account for flotation costs, proceeds to the issuing company after flotation costs have been deducted are substituted for bond price in the YTM equation.

The percentage cost of preferred stock is the rate of return required by investors in the company's preferred stock, adjusted for flotation costs incurred in selling new shares. Since preferred-stock dividends are not tax deductible to the issuing company, no tax adjustment is necessary.

- The required rate of return on preferred stock, K_p, was used in Chapter 6 to find the value of preferred stock (VP). Solving the valuation equation for K_p and adjusting for flotation costs yields the following formula for the cost of preferred stock:

$$K_p = D_p/P_{net}$$

  D_p is the annual preferred dividend and P_{net} is selling price per share minus flotation costs.

- For example, suppose a company's preferred stock has a par value of $50 per share and a dividend rate of 9 percent. New preferred stock can be sold for $43 per share. If flotation costs are $2 per share, the cost of the preferred stock is:

$$K_p = [(0.09)(\$50)]/(\$43 - \$2) = \$4.50/\$41 = 0.11, \text{ or } 11\%$$

The percentage cost of common equity is the rate of return required by investors in the company's common stock. There are two sources of common equity: retained earnings and issuance of new shares of common stock.

- Retained earnings are earnings generated by profitable operations that are not paid out as dividends to shareholders but are reinvested in the company. They are referred to as *internal equity*. The capital obtained from issuing additional shares of common stock is *external equity*. There are costs involved in using either one of these sources to raise equity capital.

Chapter 7

When earnings are retained by a company, its shareholders incur an opportunity cost by not being able to invest dividends that would otherwise have been distributed.

■ There are three methods of estimating the percentage cost of retained earnings.

Using the constant-growth model, the cost of retained earnings can be estimated as:

$$K_c = (D_1/P_0) + g$$

where D_1 = the expected dividend for next year, P_0 = the price per share of common stock, and g = the expected rate of growth in dividends. *Note that P_0 = VC in an efficient market.*

■ For example, suppose a company's common stock has a market value of $35 per share. If the company has just paid a $3.00 per share dividend and the annual growth rate in dividends is expected to be 5 percent, the cost of retained earnings is calculated as follows:

$$D_1 = (\$3.00)(1 + 0.05) = \$3.15$$

$$K_c = (\$3.15/\$35) + 0.05 = 0.09 + 0.05 = 0.14, \text{ or } 14\%$$

Note that there are no flotation costs associated with retained earnings and that common stock dividends are not tax deductible to the company.

■ The term D_1/P_0 is the stock's dividend yield. This method is sometimes called the *dividend yield plus growth rate approach.*

Another method for estimating a company's cost of retained earnings is the capital asset pricing model (CAPM). This model, introduced in Chapter 5, calculates the required rate of return as follows:

$$K_c = R_f + (K_m - R_f)\beta$$

■ Estimates of the risk-free rate of return (R_f), the required rate of return on the market portfolio (K_m), and a company's beta (β) are necessary to use this method to estimate

105

Chapter 7

the cost of retained earnings.

A third method for estimating the cost of retained earnings is to start with a company's before-tax cost of bonds and add to that a risk premium of several percentage points.

- Experience indicates that the cost of retained earnings is normally three to six percentage points higher than the before-tax cost of bonds:

$$K_c = K_d + (0.03 \text{ to } 0.06)$$

This equation can be used to check the reasonableness of the estimates of K_c found with the constant-growth model and the CAPM.

Issuing new common stock as a source of equity capital is more costly to a company than retaining earnings because of the flotation costs involved in a new stock issue.

- The constant-growth model, adjusted for flotation costs, is used to calculate the cost of new common stock (K_{nc}) as follows:

$$K_{nc} = D_1/P_{net} + g$$

where P_{net} is the price per share minus flotation costs.

Note that the only difference between the cost of new common stock and the cost of retained earnings (calculated with the constant-growth model) is the adjustment for flotation costs.

- In the example for calculating the cost of retained earnings using the constant-growth model, the stock price was $35 per share, the next annual dividend was $3.15 per share, and the growth rate in dividends was 5 percent. If the same company chooses to sell new common stock and must pay flotation costs of $4 per share, the cost of new common stock (K_{nc}) is:

$$K_{nc} = [\$3.15/(\$35 - \$4)] + 0.05 = 0.102 + 0.05 = 0.152, \text{ or } 15.2\%$$

The cost of new common stock will always be higher than the cost of retained earnings because of flotation costs.

The average cost of capital is a weighted average of the component costs of debt, preferred stock, and common equity:

$$K_a = W_i K_i + W_p K_p + W_c K_c$$

K_a = average cost of capital
K_i = after-tax cost of debt
K_p = cost of preferred stock
K_c = cost of common equity
W = weight (proportion) of total capital represented by each capital source

■ For example, suppose a company is planning to raise $3,000,000 in new long-term capital. The company wishes to raise the capital in proportions of 40 percent debt and 60 percent common equity. The estimated component costs of capital are 7 percent for debt and 12.5 percent for common equity. The average cost of capital for the company is:

$$K_a = (\$1,200,000/\$3,000,000)(0.07) + (\$1,800,000/\$3,000,000)(0.125)$$
$$= (0.40)((0.07) + (0.60)(0.125)$$
$$= 0.103, \text{ or } 10.3\%$$

Sometimes, the use of one component of capital results in an increase in the cost of another component of capital.

■ When the component costs are examined without considering the impact one component has on another, the costs being considered are *explicit costs*. The *implicit cost* of a capital component is the increase in the cost of another component as a result of using the first component.

■ The major implicit cost of debt is the increase in the cost of common equity resulting from the use of debt. The ability to borrow depends on the presence of common equity in the capital structure. Debt has a low explicit cost compared to common equity, yet firms would not be able to raise debt capital if they did not have the higher-cost equity base. The true cost of debt equals its explicit cost plus the implicit cost.

Chapter 7

- The weighted-average cost of capital automatically takes into account any prevailing implicit costs.

Financial leverage involves the use of fixed-cost sources of capital -- specifically, debt, with its fixed interest payments, and preferred stock, with its fixed dividend payments.

- Because the interest payments on debt are fixed, the interest must be paid whether or not company operations are profitable. If a firm's earnings before interest and taxes (EBIT) increase, the use of financial leverage results in an even higher percentage increase in its earnings after taxes (EAT). Unfortunately, just the opposite will occur to EAT if EBIT declines.

The debt-equity ratio measures the amount of debt per dollar of common equity.

- Increases in a company's debt-equity ratio lead to increases in financial leverage and the potential for gains and losses.

Financial risk **is the increased uncertainty surrounding earnings after taxes resulting from the use of debt financing.** *Business risk* **is the risk inherent in a company's operations without debt; in other words, it is the uncertainty surrounding earnings before interest and taxes resulting from company operations.**

- Increasing the amount of debt financing increases financial risk, which can eventually cause an increase in the firm's cost of capital.

When a company takes on so much debt that bondholders become concerned about the company's ability to service the debt, the cost of debt capital rises.

- Since bondholders have a priority claim on earnings, they normally react indifferently as companies take on reasonable amounts of debt. At high levels of debt, however, bondholders demand a higher rate of return on any new debt to compensate for the increasing risk that the issuer will default.

The cost of common equity also rises with increasing financial leverage.

- When no debt financing is used, the cost of common equity is equal to the risk-free rate of return plus a premium that reflects the company's business risk. As a company increases its use of debt financing, shareholders require a higher rate of return to compensate them for the increased financial risk they perceive. The cost of common equity rises because of the added premium for financial risk.

For a company with no debt financing, use of financial leverage initially *decreases* **the average cost of capital. At some combination of debt and equity, the average cost of capital reaches a** *minimum* **and then begins to** *increase.*

- When a company first begins to use debt financing, its average cost of capital decreases because it is using lower-cost debt, with its tax-deductible interest, instead of costly equity.

- The minimum average cost of capital identifies the *optimal capital structure*, the best mix of debt and equity. Optimal capital structure maximizes the value of the company and the price of its common stock because it minimizes the discount rate used to find the present value of the company's cash flows.

- At debt-equity ratios beyond the optimal capital structure, the average cost of capital increases rapidly. The increased possibility of financial distress associated with high debt levels causes both bondholders and common shareholders to require higher rates of return, resulting in a higher average cost of capital. The higher average cost of capital leads to a decline in company value and the price of common stock.

The *marginal cost of capital (MCC)* **is the percentage cost of the last dollar of capital raised by a company during a planning period. MCC is equal to or greater than the average cost of capital.**

- The cost of capital may increase as the dollar size of the capital budget increases for two reasons: (1) when companies use up available retained earnings, they must issue new common stock as their source of equity financing, and the cost of new common stock is always greater than the cost of retained earnings because of flotation costs; and (2) the cost of debt may increase as a company takes on more and more debt.

The cost of the final increment of capital raised *in optimal proportions* **of debt and equity is the marginal cost of capital.**

Chapter 7

- For example, suppose the $3,000,000 investment planned by the company in the example at the beginning of the chapter outline consists of three different projects with the following costs:

$$\text{Project A} = \$1,000,000$$
$$\text{Project B} = \$1,500,000$$
$$\text{Project C} = \$500,000$$

The costs of the capital components are as follows:

K_i = 7% for amounts up to and including $1,000,000
K_i = 8% for amounts exceeding $1,000,000
K_c = 12.5%
K_{nc} = 13.8%

Retained earnings are estimated to be $600,000, and capital will be raised in the optimal proportions of 40 percent debt and 60 percent equity.

Project A could be financed using the $600,000 in retained earnings and borrowing the remaining $400,000. The marginal cost of capital is:

$$K_a = (0.40)(0.07) + (0.60)(0.125)$$
$$= 0.103, \text{ or } 10.3\%$$

In order to also finance Project B, the company must issue $900,000 in new common stock since 60 percent of its financing must come from an equity source and the company's retained earnings were exhausted on Project A. The other $600,000 needed would come from debt financing. Thus, the marginal cost of capital here is:

$$K_a = (0.40)(0.07) + (0.60)(0.138)$$
$$= 0.111, \text{ or } 11.1\%$$

To invest in all three projects, the company needs an additional $500,000, the cost of Project C. The equity portion, $300,000, must again be furnished by new common stock since retained earnings were exhausted on Project A. The $200,000 debt financing needed will cost 8 percent now instead of 7 percent because the total amount borrowed on A, B, and C will exceed $1,000,000.

The marginal cost of investing in all three projects is:

$$K_a = (0.40)(0.08) + (0.60)(0.138)$$
$$= 0.115, \text{ or } 11.5\%$$

■ The *marginal cost of capital schedule* is a line depicting the cost of capital for various increments of capital.

Financial managers use MCC in capital budgeting -- the process of evaluating and selecting capital projects.

■ For an average-risk project to be accepted by a company, its expected rate of return must exceed MCC. If expected return is less than MCC, the project should be rejected because investing in it will lower shareholder wealth.

Estimating a company's average and marginal cost of capital is easier to do in theory than in practice. Some of the difficulties encountered include:

■ The weights used in calculating average and marginal cost of capital may be based on *book value* or *market value*. Market value weights are preferable because they reflect investors' current attitudes about the value of the firm.

■ In the short-term, it may be difficult for companies to raise capital in proportions that preserve the optimal capital structure. They frequently issue common stock one year and bonds the next, continually moving away from and back toward the optimal capital structure.

■ The average and marginal cost of capital normally include only long-term debt and equity. Some companies use short-term financing as a permanent source of capital. If the amount is significant, its cost should be included in the calculation of the cost of capital.

■ For some projects, financial managers may seek *project-specific financing* instead of financing with optimal debt-equity ratios. This normally becomes an issue for large investment projects in lines of business differing from the company's existing business.

Financial managers should consider several criteria before selecting a financing

Chapter 7

alternative:

- *Cost*. Assess the component cost of each source of long-term financing and be wary of relying exclusively on one source.

- *Risk*. From the company's viewpoint, the risk of the securities stems from the legal obligations they create.

- *Control*. With stock financing, current shareholders may suffer *dilution of control* unless they purchase some of the new stock.

- *Maneuverability*. The type of financing used today influences a company's future *financial maneuverability*, the ability to move at will between debt and equity financing.

GLOSSARY OF KEY TERMS

average cost of capital: weighted average of the component costs of capital
book weights: proportions of long-term capital sources based on book values
business risk: uncertainty surrounding future earnings before interest and taxes as a result of company operations
capital budgeting: evaluating and selecting capital investments for a planning period
capital project: capital expenditure, or capital investment; project usually involving depreciable assets that generate cash flows over several years
component cost of capital: estimated percentage cost of a component -- bonds, preferred stock, new common stock, and retained earnings -- in a company's capital structure
cost of bonds: investors' required rate of return on bonds, adjusted for flotation costs and the tax deductibility of interest payments
cost of capital: percentage cost a company pays for funds to finance its investments

cost of new common stock: investors' required rate of return on the company's common stock, adjusted for flotation costs

cost of preferred stock: investors' required rate of return on the preferred stock, adjusted for flotation costs

cost of retained earnings: shareholders' required rate of return on the company's common stock

debt capacity: amount of debt with which a specific project optimally should be financed

debt-equity ratio: amount of debt per dollar of common equity

earnings available to common shareholders: amount of earnings after taxes and preferred-stock dividends have been paid by the company

explicit cost: percentage cost of a source of capital without regard to its impact on the cost of another component

external equity: financing generated from the issuance of new common stock

financial leverage: use of a fixed-cost source of capital, e.g., debt or preferred stock

financial risk: possibility that actual earnings after taxes will differ from their expected value because a company uses debt financing

implicit cost: change in the percentage cost of a source of capital resulting from the use of another source

internal equity: financing generated within a company from the retention of earnings

marginal cost of capital (MCC): cost of the final increment of capital raised in optimal proportions of debt and equity

marginal cost of capital schedule: line depicting the cost of capital for various increments of capital

market weights: proportions of long-term capital sources based on market values

optimal capital structure: debt-equity ratio that minimizes a company's cost of capital and maximizes its stock price

yield-to-maturity: average annual rate of return investors expect to receive on a bond by holding it to maturity

Chapter 7

MULTIPLE CHOICE SELF-TEST

1. Which of the following are sources of common equity to a firm?

    a. new shares of preferred stock
    b. retained earnings
    c. new shares of common stock
    d. a and c
    e. b and c

2. When using the CAPM to estimate the cost of retained earnings, which of the following would lead to an increase in K_c?

    a. an increase in beta
    b. investors become less risk-averse
    c. expected inflation decreases
    d. the SML becomes flatter
    e. all of the above would cause an increase in K_c

3. The cost of new common stock financing (K_{nc}) is generally

    a. lower than the cost of retained earnings
    b. the same as the cost of retained earnings
    c. higher than the cost of retained earnings
    d. more stable than the cost of retained earnings
    e. preferred to the cost of retained earnings

4. The predominant source of financial leverage is

    a. debt
    b. preferred stock
    c. retained earnings
    d. common stock
    e. all are major sources of financial leverage

Chapter 7

5. Financial leverage used by a company is measured with the

   a. interest-capital ratio
   b. debt-equity ratio
   c. assets-earnings ratio
   d. earnings per share
   e. earnings before interest and taxes

6. Compared to common shareholders, bondholders' claims are

   a. longer
   b. inferior
   c. trivial
   d. insupportable
   e. senior

7. The average cost of capital

   a. always decreases as the debt-equity ratio increases
   b. is weighted by the proportions of the various sources of capital
   c. is not used in evaluating capital projects
   d. contains only implicit costs
   e. is maximized at the optimal capital structure

8. The optimal capital structure

   a. maximizes earnings per share
   b. minimizes total interest expense
   c. maximizes price per share of common stock
   d. minimizes the cost of equity
   e. eliminates financial risk

Chapter 7

9. In calculating the marginal cost of capital, the financial manager should use

    a. market weights of the capital components
    b. book weights of the capital components
    c. the risk-free rate of return
    d. a risk-adjusted discount rate
    e. the average of book and market weights

10. A capital project of average risk should be accepted if its expected return exceeds

    a. the incremental cost of debt
    b. the rate of return on existing projects
    c. the marginal cost of capital
    d. management's projections
    e. the cost of new common stock

11. Which of the following factors can financial managers safely ignore when evaluating alternative financing plans?

    a. cost
    b. risk
    c. possible dilution of shareholder control
    d. financial maneuverability
    e. all must be considered

Chapter 7

PROBLEMS

1. Find the after-tax cost of bonds for a firm whose bonds are currently selling for $905.50. The bonds carry a 12 percent coupon, paid semiannually, and mature in 8 years at $1,000. Assume a 40 percent marginal tax rate and ignore flotation costs.

2. Find the cost of preferred stock for Raven Co., which can issue new shares at $50 per share. Flotation costs are $2.50 per share, and the dividend on the stock is $7.50 per share.

3. B&B Appliances has experienced a 6 percent decline in earnings and dividends during each of the past 5 years, and this rate of decline is expected to continue indefinitely. An annual dividend of $3.50 per share was paid two days ago. If the current price of the stock is $18.00 per share, what is B&B's cost of retained earnings?

4. Calculate the cost of retained earnings for a firm with a beta of 0.85 if the return on the S&P 500 is 10 percent and U.S. Treasury bonds are yielding 6 percent.

5. ZMM Enterprises estimates its cost of retained earnings by adding 5 percentage points to its before-tax cost of bonds. ZMM's bonds have the following features: $1,000 par, semiannual interest, 9.5 percent coupon, and 7 years to maturity. The bonds are priced at $1,079.22. Use the approximate YTM equation to arrive at an estimate of the cost of retained earnings for ZMM.

6. Borrocks Company can sell new shares of common stock for $16.50 per share. Flotation costs involved in issuing the stock are 10 percent. Borrock's earnings and dividends are growing at an annual rate of 5 percent, and this level is expected to continue indefinitely. The last dividend paid was $2.20 per share. Calculate K_{nc}.

Use the following information to answer problems 7 through 12:

RJW Corporation expects to finance several proposed projects with a combination of bonds, preferred stock, retained earnings, and common stock. Management wants to maintain the current capital structure, which is considered optimal. Based on current

Chapter 7

conditions in the capital market, RJW's financial manager prepared the following information:

Source of Funds	Par Value	Interest or Dividend Rate	Proceeds per Security
Bonds (10-yr. maturity)	$1,000	9%	$937.70
Preferred stock	100	9%	$ 86.20
Common stock	10		$ 92.00

The values of RJW's outstanding debt and equity are as follows:

		Book Value	Market Value
Bonds		$ 650,000	$ 705,000
Preferred stock		150,000	176,000
Common stock	$ 210,420		
Paid in capital	720,000		
Retained earnings	1,039,580		
Total common equity		1,970,000	2,020,000
Total capital		$2,770,000	$2,901,000

RJW's common stock currently trades at $96 per share. Current dividends are $4.00 per share and are expected to grow at a constant annual rate of 8 percent. Next year's addition to retained earnings is forecasted to be $450,000, and the marginal tax rate is 34 percent.

7. Calculate RJW's component cost of bonds.

8. Calculate RJW's component cost of preferred stock.

9. Calculate RJW's component cost of retained earnings.

10. Calculate RJW's component cost of new common stock.

11. What is the maximum budget supportable by RJW's expected retained earnings?

12. Calculate the marginal cost of capital if RJW's capital budget is $700,000 for the coming year.

Chapter 7

Use the following information to answer problems 13 through 17.

Rusty Steele Products (RSP) had $80,000,000 in total assets at the end of last year. RSP plans to acquire $20,000,000 in new machinery this year. Bonds can be issued to yield 8 percent per year. Common stock currently trades at $30 per share. Flotation costs for issuing new common stock equal $3 per share. RSP expects to retain $5,000,000 of earnings this year. RSP's most recent common stock dividend was $1.50 per share; investors expect the dividend to grow indefinitely at 6 percent per year. The company's marginal tax rate is 34 percent, and the following capital structure is considered optimal:

	Market Value
Bonds	$30,000,000
Common equity	50,000,000

13. What is RSP's after-tax cost of debt?

14. What is RSP's cost of retained earnings?

15. What is RSP's cost of new common stock?

16. What is the maximum capital budget supportable by RSP's retained earnings?

17. Calculate RSP's marginal cost of capital for its $20,000,000 budget.

SOLUTIONS TO MULTIPLE CHOICE SELF-TEST

1. e   7. b
2. a   8. c
3. c   9. a
4. a   10. c
5. b   11. e
6. e

Chapter 7

SOLUTIONS TO PROBLEMS

1. $K_i = K_d(1 - T)$

   $K_d = ?$
   $I/2 = (0.12 \times \$1,000)/2 = \$60$
   $2n = (2)(8) = 16$

   $\$905.50 = (\$60)([1-(1+k_d/2)^{-16}]/(k_d/2)) + (\$1,000)(1+k_d/2)^{-16}$
   If $k_d/2 = 7\%$: $(\$60)(9.4466) + (\$1,000)(0.3387)$
   $= \$566.80 + \$338.70$
   $= \$905.50$

   YTM $= 7\% \times 2 = 14\%$

   $K_i = 14\%(1 - 0.40) = 8.4\%$

2. $K_p = D_p/P_{net}$
   $= \$7.50/(\$50.00 - \$2.50)$
   $= \$7.50/\$47.50$
   $= 0.158$, or 15.8%

3. $K_c = (D_1/P_0) + g$

   $D_1 = D_0(1 + g)$
   $= \$3.50(1 - .06)$
   $= \$3.29$
   $K_c = (\$3.29/\$18.00) + (-0.06)$
   $= 0.1228$, or 12.28%

4. $K_c = R_f + (K_m - R_f)\beta$
   $= 6\% + (10\% - 6\%)(0.85)$
   $= 9.4\%$

5. Approx. YTM = $\{I + [(Par-VB)/n]\}/[(VB+Par)/2]$

   = $\{\$95 + [(\$1{,}000 - \$1{,}079.22)/7]\}/[(\$1{,}079.22 + \$1{,}000)/2]$
   = $\$83.68/\$1{,}039.61$
   = 0.080, or 8%

   $K_c = K_d + 5\%$
   $ = 8\% + 5\%$
   $ = 13\%$

6. $K_{nc} = (D_1/P_{net}) + g$

   $D_1 = D_0(1 + g)$
   $ = \$2.20(1 + 0.05)$
   $ = \$2.31$

   $P_{net} = \$16.50 - [(0.10)(\$16.50)] = \$14.85$

   $K_{nc} = (\$2.31/\$14.85) + 0.05$
   $\phantom{K_{nc}} = 0.2056$, or 20.56%

7. $K_i = K_d(1 - T)$
   $K_d = YTM$
   YTM = discount rate that equates PV of cash flows to price

   $I/2 = (0.09 \times \$1{,}000)/2 = \$90/2 = \$45$
   $2n = (2)(10) = 20$ semiannual time periods

   $\$937.70 = (\$45)[1-(1+k_d/2)^{-20}]/(k_d/2)) + (\$1{,}000)(1+k_d/2)^{-20}$

   Through trial and error, one finds that a discount rate of 5% makes the PV of cash flows equal to the bond's price:

   $\$937.70 = (\$45)(12.4622) + (\$1{,}000)(0.3769)$
   $ = \$560.80 + \$376.90$
   $ = \$937.70$

Chapter 7

$$YTM = 0.05 \times 2 = 0.10$$
$$K_i = (0.10)(1 - 0.34)$$
$$= 0.066, \text{ or } 6.6\%$$

8. $K_p = D_p/P_{net}$
   $= (0.09 \times \$100)/\$86.20$
   $= \$9.00/\$86.20$
   $= 0.104, \text{ or } 10.4\%$

9. $K_c = (D_1/P_0) + g$

   $D_1 = D_0(1 + g)$
   $= \$4.00(1 + 0.08)$
   $= \$4.32$

   $K_c = (\$4.32/\$96.00) + 0.08$
   $= 0.045 + 0.08$
   $= 0.125, \text{ or } 12.5\%$

10. $K_{nc} = (D_1/P_{net}) + g$
    $= (\$4.32/\$92.00) + 0.08$
    $= 0.047 + 0.08$
    $= 0.127, \text{ or } 12.7\%$

11. Using market values, equity % = \$2,020,000/\$2,901,000
    $= 0.696, \text{ or } 69.6\%$

    Maximum budget = Retained earnings/Equity %
    $= \$450,000/0.696$
    $= \$646,552$

12. $MCC = W_i K_i + W_p K_p + W_c K_c$

    Note that since planned budget of \$700,000 exceeds maximum supportable by retained earnings (\$646,552), new common stock will have to be issued. Thus, K_{nc} in place of K_c is used in MCC equation.

Market Weights:
$W_i = \$705,000/\$2,901,000 = 0.243$

$W_p = \$176,000/\$2,901,000 = 0.061$

$W_c = \$2,020,000/\$2,901,000 = \underline{0.696}$
1.000

$MCC = (0.243)(0.066) + (0.061)(0.104) + (0.696)(0.127)$
$ = 0.016 + 0.006 + 0.088$
$ = 0.11$, or 11%

13. $K_i = K_d(1 - T)$
    $ = (0.08)(1 - 0.34)$
    $ = 0.528$, or 5.28%

14. $K_c = (D_1/P_0) + g$

    $D_1 = D_0(1 + g)$
    $ = \$1.50(1 + 0.06)$
    $ = \$1.59$

    $K_c = (\$1.59/\$30) + 0.06$
    $ = 0.053 + 0.06$
    $ = 0.113$, or 11.3%

15. $K_{nc} = (D_1/P_{net}) + g$
    $\phantom{K_{nc}} = (\$1.59/\$27) + 0.06$
    $\phantom{K_{nc}} = 0.059 + 0.06$
    $\phantom{K_{nc}} = 0.119$, or 11.9%

16. Equity % $= \$50,000,000/\$80,000,000$
    $ = 0.625$, or 62.5%

    Maximum budget $=$ Retained earnings/Equity %
    $ = \$5,000,000/0.625$
    $ = \$8,000,000$

Chapter 7

17. $MCC = W_i K_i + W_c K_c$

    $W_i = \$30{,}000{,}000/\$80{,}000{,}00 = 0.375$
    $W_c = \$50{,}000{,}000/\$80{,}000{,}000 = 0.625$

    Note that since the planned budget is $20,000,000 and retained earnings will only support a budget of $8,000,000, new common stock must be issued. Thus, K_{nc} in place of K_c is used in the MCC.

    $MCC = (0.375)(0.0528) + (0.625)(0.119)$
    $ = 0.0198 + 0.0744$
    $ = 0.942$, or 9.42%

8 CAPITAL INVESTMENTS and CASH FLOWS

OVERVIEW

One of the tasks of the financial manager discussed in Chapter 1 was the process of deciding which assets the company should own -- the *investment decision*. Financial managers analyze different capital investment opportunities and recommend action to be taken by the company. Because these investments typically involve large cash outlays and last for many years, errors in the evaluation process can produce serious consequences. Evaluation and selection of capital investments are fundamental to the success or failure of a company, and it is essential that the evaluation process be done carefully. This chapter examines the way financial managers calculate the relevant *cash flows* associated with a capital investment, paying special attention to the impact of depreciation and taxes. Chapter 9 will present methods financial managers can use to evaluate a project's expected cash flows.

OUTLINE

The process of evaluating and selecting capital investment projects is called *capital budgeting*.

- Capital investments, also called capital expenditures or capital projects, usually involve the purchase of a depreciable asset.

The capital budgeting process consists of the following steps:

Chapter 8

- *Generate ideas* for projects. The ideas may come from many sources, such as planning committees, research and development groups, vendors, customers, or individual employees.

- *Estimate the cash outflows and inflows* associated with each project.

- *Evaluate the risks* of each proposal, assessing the uncertainty of both the required cash outlay and the estimated cash inflows.

- *Select projects* that are expected to increase the company's stock price.

- *Monitor accepted projects* for variance from expected performance.

Ideally, methods used to evaluate the acceptability of proposed projects should include the following factors:

- Take into account all incremental cash flows occurring over the entire life of the proposed project.

- Incorporate the principle of time value of money.

- Recognize and incorporate the project's required rate of return.

The relevant cash flows in capital budgeting are those directly attributable to the project.

- *Changes* in the company's cash flows resulting from acceptance of a project are what is relevant in the capital budgeting process. These changes are called *incremental cash flows*.

- Incremental cash flows should include any *indirect cash flows*, which are cash inflows and outflows that occur in other parts of a company's operations as a result of the company investing in a particular project.

- Nonincremental cash flows such as *sunk costs* are not relevant in the capital budgeting process. Sunk costs are cash outlays a company has already made or is legally committed to make, regardless of whether or not the project under consideration is

Chapter 8

accepted.

There are three principal types of incremental cash flows associated with capital projects:

>Net investment cash outflow
>Operating cash flows
>Disposal cash flow

The net investment cash outflow (NICO) represents the expenditure required to put the project into operation. It usually consists of cash outflows to acquire depreciable assets and additional net working capital requirements. The following factors are considered in the calculation of NICO:

- Cost of the depreciable asset(s) involved in the project.

- Any additional costs necessary to bring the asset on line are added to the cost of the asset for calculation of NICO. (These additional costs are also added to purchase price when calculating an investment tax credit or depreciation expense.) Examples include delivery charges and installation costs.

- Some asset purchases may be eligible for an *investment tax credit (ITC)*. This is a percentage stipulated by the U.S. Congress that, in effect, reduces the cost of investing in certain types of capital assets. The purpose of granting an investment tax credit is to boost the economy by encouraging capital investment. If an asset is eligible for an investment tax credit, the ITC percentage is multiplied times the full cost of the asset (cost plus delivery, installation, etc.). The amount of the credit is netted out against the cost of the asset in calculating NICO. In reality, the ITC, like other tax credits, directly reduces the company's tax liability. Congress repealed the ITC in 1986, but it may resurface again.

- Sometimes, additional *net working capital (NWC)* is required to support a capital project. Net working capital is equal to current assets minus current liabilities. A project may require an additional investment in current assets that may not be covered by a corresponding increase in current liabilities. The incremental increase in the net working capital caused by undertaking a project is considered a cash outflow under NICO.

Chapter 8

To summarize, NICO is the sum of the following cash outflows and inflows:

- Cost of asset -- *outflow*

- Delivery charges, installation costs, etc. -- *outflow*

- Investment tax credit -- *inflow*

- Increase in net working capital -- *outflow*

Operating cash flows (OCF) are generated during the operating life of the project. They result from (1) an increase in sales that exceeds any increase in expenses, or (2) a reduction in expenses with no corresponding effect on sales. These operating cash flows must be adjusted for taxes and depreciation effects.

- The existence of corporate income taxes reduces the size of operating cash flows. The *marginal tax rate* is the tax rate applied to the last, or marginal, dollar of taxable income. A company's *average tax rate* is simply its total taxes paid divided by its taxable income. In capital budgeting, financial managers use the marginal tax rate to evaluate incremental cash flows.

Depreciation **is a periodic charge taken against the cost of a capital asset so as to allocate that cost over a specified number of years, instead of taking the whole charge in one year. The U.S. tax code lists class lives for assets, which represent the number of years over which an asset may be depreciated for tax purposes. Class life may differ from the expected life of a proposed project.**

- The reason depreciation is so important to companies is because it is a *noncash* operating expense. Depreciation reduces taxable income and therefore the amount of taxes a company must pay, but it does not represent an actual cash outflow. Thus, depreciation increases after-tax cash flow by lowering taxes paid.

- For tax purposes, companies are required to calculate depreciation using one of two methods: *modified accelerated cost recovery system (MACRS)* or *straight-line depreciation*. Other methods are allowable for financial reporting purposes, but for tax purposes, and therefore capital budgeting, one of these two methods must be used.

Chapter 8

MACRS is an accelerated form of depreciation, meaning that a company writes off more of the depreciable asset in the early years than it would with straight-line depreciation. This larger write-off in early years generates higher present values of tax savings, making MACRS the most commonly- used method for tax purposes.

- Because of the complexity in calculating depreciation rates under MACRS, the IRS publishes tables listing the rates for different asset class lives. Once the appropriate class life has been determined, the corresponding percentage from the table is multiplied by the full depreciable cost of the asset to determine the annual depreciation expense.

   Note that salvage value is not deducted from the depreciable base when using MACRS.

- The MACRS rates include an adjustment for the *half-year convention*, which is a U.S. tax code requirement that a company take a half-year's depreciation in the year of acquisition and a half-year's depreciation in the year following the class life. When looking at a table of MACRS rates, one notices that there are percentages listed for 4 years under the 3-year class life, 6 years under the 5-year class life, and so on. This is because of the half-year convention.

Straight-line depreciation requires the allocation of equal annual percentages of an asset's historical cost over the asset's class life.

- Historical cost includes purchase price, delivery charges, and installation costs. The annual depreciation rate is 1/class life. Again, class life is determined by the U.S. tax code, not by the project's useful life. The annual rate is multiplied by the historical cost to find the annual depreciation expense.

   Note that salvage value is not deducted from historical cost when using straight-line depreciation for tax purposes.

- When using straight-line depreciation, the financial manager must make the adjustment for the half-year convention discussed above. One half of the annual amount must be taken in the first year of class life and one half is taken in the year following the last year of class life.

Operating cash flows (OCF) may be calculated using an operating cash flow

Chapter 8

statement or the following equation:

$$OCF = \text{Earnings after taxes} + \text{Depreciation}$$

■ Both methods begin with assessing any change that will occur in the company's sales if a project is accepted. Subtracted from any change in sales is any change in operating expenses, including depreciation. The result is earnings before interest and taxes (EBIT).

■ Interest expense is *not* included in OCF because the cost of financing the asset (whatever the source of financing) is included in the weighted-average cost of capital, which will be used as the discount rate in calculating the present value of the OCF. Including interest expense in OCF (if the project were to be financed by debt) would be double counting.

■ Once the relevant EBIT has been determined, taxes are calculated and deducted, resulting in earnings after taxes (EAT). *Note that EAT is not the same as OCF.* The depreciation expense that had been deducted to calculate taxable income must be added back in to determine OCF since depreciation did not involve an actual cash outflow. Thus, OCF is equal to EAT plus depreciation.

■ Operating cash flows must be calculated for each year of a proposed project's operating life. Note again that operating life may differ from class life, but it is the number of years of operating life that determine OCF. Class life is used strictly for depreciation purposes.

In capital budgeting, projects are assumed to have a finite life. The final set of cash flows involved are the cash flows associated with terminating a project, often referred to as disposal cash flows.

■ One component of disposal cash flows is the net proceeds obtained from the sale or disposal of depreciable assets. Whenever a company disposes of an asset, there are tax consequences to be considered. The market value of the asset must be compared to the asset's book value. Book value, equal to historical cost minus accumulated depreciation, represents uncharged depreciation or historical cost still on the company's books.

Chapter 8

If market value > book value, there is a gain, and the company must pay taxes on the gain. The amount of taxes owed is equal to the gain times the company's marginal tax rate.

If market value < book value, the company incurs a loss. The loss results in tax savings for the company. The amount of tax savings is found by multiplying the loss times the company's marginal tax rate.

- The other component of disposal cash flows is the recovery of net working capital as the company liquidates the project's current assets and pays the project's current liabilities. As a practical matter, financial managers assume that current assets will be liquidated at book value. Thus, any increase in NWC that was charged as a cash outflow under NICO will be recovered as a cash inflow under disposal cash flows.

To summarize, disposal cash flows are the sum of the following inflows and outflows:

- Proceeds from the sale (disposal) of the asset at the end of its operating life -- *inflow*

- If asset is sold for a gain, taxes owed -- *outflow*

- If asset is sold for a loss, tax savings -- *inflow*

- Recovery of increase in net working capital -- *inflow*

The following example will illustrate the calculation of incremental cash flows in the capital budgeting process:

Micromania Computers, Inc. is evaluating a new process to manufacture printed circuit boards. The project will involve the purchase of new equipment for $474,000. Delivery and installation charges will total an additional $6,000. Assume the equipment is eligible for a 10 percent investment tax credit.

Although the project has a 4-year useful life, the new equipment has a 3-year class life and will be depreciated on a straight-line basis. Net working capital will increase by $33,000 if the project is undertaken. It is expected that the company will be able to sell the equipment for $50,000 at the end of its 4-year life.

Chapter 8

Incremental sales are forecast at $400,000 in the first year, increasing by 20 percent over each of the following three years. Incremental overhead and rent expenses due to the project are expected to be $75,000 annually. Variable costs are estimated at 40 percent of sales. Micromania has an average tax rate of 28 percent and a marginal tax rate of 34 percent.

Calculate all incremental cash flows associated with the project.

Step One: Net Investment Cash Outflow

Purchase price	$474,000
Delivery and installation charges	6,000
Investment tax credit (10% x $480,000)	(48,000)
Increase in net working capital	33,000
Net investment cash outflow	$465,000

Step Two: Depreciation

Straight-line depreciation = Historical cost/Class life
= $480,000/3
= $160,000 annual rate

With the half-year adjustment, annual depreciation expense is
Year 1 = $80,000
Year 2 = $160,000
Year 3 = $160,000
Year 4 = $80,000

To check that the half-year adjustment is correct, sum the annual charges to make sure they equal the historical cost.

Step Three: Operating Cash Flows

OCF = (Sales - VC - FC - Depreciation)(1 - T) + Depreciation

OCF_1 = ($400,000 - $160,000 - $75,000 - $80,000)(1 - 0.34) + $80,000

= $136,100

OCF_2 = ($480,000 - $192,000 - $75,000 - $160,000)(1 - 0.34) + $160,000
= $194,980

OCF_3 = ($576,000 - $230,400 - $75,000 - $160,000)(1 - 0.34) + $160,000
= $232,996

OCF_4 = ($691,200 - $276,480 - $75,000 - $80,000)(1 - 0.34) + $80,000
= $251,415

Step Four: Disposal Cash Flow

Proceeds from sale of equipment		$50,000
Tax consequences		
Market value	$50,000	
Book value	0	
Gain on sale	$50,000	
Taxes owed	× 0.34	(17,000)
Recovery of net working capital		33,000
Disposal cash flow		$66,000

Note that two cash flows are assumed to occur at the end of year 4:

    $251,415 operating cash flows
+ $ 66,000 disposal cash flows
= $317,415 total year 4 cash flows

Chapter 8

GLOSSARY OF KEY TERMS

average tax rate: tax rate applied to the average dollar of taxable income; total taxes paid divided by taxable income

class life: number of years over which an asset may be depreciated for tax purposes

depreciable asset: property on which the U.S. tax code permits a company to charge depreciation against income

depreciable basis: portion of asset value that can be depreciated for tax purposes

half-year convention: U.S. tax code requirement that a company take a half-year's depreciation in the year of acquisition and a half-year's depreciation in the year following the last year of class life

historical cost: acquisition cost of a depreciable asset consisting of its purchase price plus delivery charges and installation costs

incremental cash flows: changes in a company's cash flows attributable to a capital investment

indirect cash flows: incremental cash flows in parts of a company other than the capital project, but caused by the capital project

investment tax credit (ITC): percentage of the cost of a depreciable asset that the U.S. tax code allows as a reduction in a company's tax bill; repealed in 1986

marginal tax rate: tax rate applied to the last, or marginal, dollar of taxable income

modified accelerated cost recovery system (MACRS): Congressionally imposed depreciation procedures for tax purposes

net investment cash outflow (NICO): capital expenditure to get a capital project in working order; typically includes expenditures for depreciable assets and net working capital

net working capital: current assets minus current liabilities

straight-line depreciation: depreciation method requiring allocation of equal percentages of an asset's historical cost over the asset's class life

sunk cost: cash outlay that cannot be recouped and therefore is not attributable to a capital project

tax shelter: a noncash, tax-deductible expense; also known as tax shield

Chapter 8

MULTIPLE CHOICE SELF-TEST

1. The cash flows relevant to the evaluation of a capital investment project are

   a. incremental
   b. indefinable
   c. inconsequential
   d. infinite
   e. certain

2. Relevant cash flows for a capital project should be estimated

   a. as a percent of sales
   b. on an after-tax basis
   c. using accrual methods
   d. at the end of the project
   e. only if known with certainty

3. Ideas for investment in new capital projects can come from

   a. planning committees
   b. customers
   c. vendors
   d. individual employees
   e. all of the above

4. Capital projects sometimes contribute to a company's cash flows by

   a. increasing sales
   b. reducing expenses
   c. reducing taxes
   d. all of the above
   e. none of the above

135

Chapter 8

5. The tax rate applied to taxable income from a proposed project is

    a. the company's average tax rate
    b. the company's marginal tax rate
    c. the maximum corporate tax rate
    d. the investment tax credit rate
    e. the company's cost of capital

6. Which of the following cannot be included in the depreciable base of an asset?

    a. purchase price
    b. shipping charges
    c. handling charges
    d. installation charges
    e. all of the above are included

7. Which of the following depreciation methods allows the subtraction of salvage value from purchase price?

    a. MACRS
    b. straight-line when used for financial reporting purposes
    c. straight-line when used for tax reporting purposes
    d. all of the above
    e. none of the above

8. The use of MACRS depreciation instead of straight-line depreciation

    a. may result in an asset being fully depreciated in fewer years
    b. will result in lower cash flows in the early years of a profitable asset's life
    c. will result in lower taxes in the early years of a profitable asset's life
    d. may result in the loss of the half-year convention
    e. makes the straight-line switch impossible

Chapter 8

9. The calculation of the net investment cash outflow associated with a proposed capital project should include

    a. annual depreciation
    b. increases in net working capital
    c. changes in sales revenue
    d. sunk costs
    e. the expected change in stock price

10. Of the two methods described in the text, the one used for calculating operating cash flows depends on

    a. the marginal tax rate
    b. the timing of the cash flows
    c. the rate of inflation
    d. the size of the NICO
    e. personal preference

11. If a proposed project requires an increase in net working capital, which cash flows would be affected?

    a. net investment cash outflow
    b. operating cash flows
    c. project disposal cash flows
    d. a and c
    e. all of the above

12. Which of the following statements is not true?

    a. If an asset is sold for a price greater than its book value, the company will owe taxes on the amount of the gain.
    b. If an asset is sold for a price lower than its book value, the company will realize tax savings because of the loss.
    c. If an asset is scrapped and no proceeds are realized from its disposal, there is no tax effect even if the asset still has a book value.
    d. If an asset is sold for a price equal to its book value, there is no tax effect.
    e. none of the above

137

Chapter 8

PROBLEMS

1. Bursting Balloon Company (BBC) is purchasing gas cylinders for $10,000 plus $1,200 in freight charges. Depreciation will be calculated using straight-line with the half-year convention and a 3-year class life. Inventory of $3,000 is required and trade credit of $2,200 is available. Calculate NICO.

2. BBC in Problem 1 expects added revenues of $1,900 and cash operating expenses of $1,400 per month. Assuming BBC's tax rate is 40%, find the first year's operating cash flow.

3. If the cylinders in Problem 1 are sold at the end of 4 years for $5,600, and the net working capital is recovered at book value, what is the disposal cash flow for BBC?

4. Al's Auto Parts bought a $50,000 truck with a 5-year class life. The company uses MACRS depreciation. After 5 years, the truck is sold for $5,000. Al's has a 40 percent marginal tax rate. Calculate Al's tax liability as a result of the sale.

5. The financial manager of Deep Drilling, Inc. has estimated that a new drilling machine will generate additional cash sales of $400,000 and additional cash operating expenses of $240,000 next year. Depreciation expense on the new machine is $60,000 per year, and interest expense on additional financing is $36,000. Deep Drilling's marginal tax rate is 34 percent. Calculate the annual operating cash flow from the proposed drilling machine.

6. Assume that the drilling machine in Problem 5 has an original cost of $800,000 and that depreciation is calculated using MACRS and a 5-year class life. If the drilling machine is sold at the end of six years for $200,000, what will be the company's tax liability resulting from the sale?

7. Carson Textiles is considering the purchase of a new loom. It will cost $450,000, plus a $50,000 charge to have it shipped from Germany. The machine is eligible for an 8 percent investment tax credit. A spare parts inventory costing $15,000 will be required to keep the machine running; $8,000 in trade credit is available to finance the inventory. Calculate the net investment cash outflow for this proposed purchase.

Chapter 8

8. A company is planning to purchase a machine for $175,000. It will be depreciated using MACRS and a 5-year class life. The company expects the machine to last for 8 years, at which time it will be scrapped. Use of the machine will save the company $40,000 each year in cash expenses. If the company's marginal tax rate is 40 percent, what is the operating cash flow for year 7 of the project's life?

9. DJS Enterprises is planning to purchase a machine that will enable it to speed up production and delivery, thereby increasing sales. The annual increase in sales is expected to be $60,000. Cash operating expenses will increase by $10,000 each year. The machine, which is expected to last for 3 years, has a purchase price of $125,000 and will be depreciated using MACRS and a 3-year class life. The company's marginal tax rate is 40 percent. What are the annual cash flows from operations for this project?

10. Suppose DJS in Problem 9 can sell the machine after 3 years for $9,000. What are the net proceeds from the sale?

SOLUTIONS TO MULTIPLE CHOICE SELF-TEST

1. a   7. b
2. b   8. c
3. e   9. b
4. d   10. e
5. b   11. d
6. e   12. c

Chapter 8

SOLUTIONS TO PROBLEMS

1. | | | |
    |---|---|---|
    | Purchase price | $10,000 | |
    | Freight | 1,200 | |
    | Total equipment cost | | $11,200 |
    | | | |
    | Increase in current assets | $3,000 | |
    | Increase in current liabilities | (2,200) | |
    | Increase in net working capital | | 800 |
    | | | |
    | Net investment cash outflow | | $12,000 |

2. Depreciation = $11,200/3 = $3,733
    Year 1 depreciation = (0.50)($3,733) = $1,867

    Annual sales = 12($1,900) = $22,800
    Annual cash expenses = 12($1,400) = $16,800

    OCF = ($22,800 - $16,800 - $1,867)(1 - 0.40) + $1,867
    = $4,347

3. Market value $5,600
    Book value   0
    Gain on sale $5,600

    Taxes owed = ($5,600)(0.40) = $2,240

Proceeds from sale	$5,600
Taxes owed	(2,240)
Recovery of NWC	800
Disposal cash flow	$4,160

4. | | |
    |---|---|
    | Market value | $5,000 |
    | Book value (0.0576)($50,000) | 2,880 |
    | Gain on sale | $2,120 |

    Taxes owed = ($2,120)(0.40) = $848

5. OCF = ($400,000 - $240,000 - $60,000)(1 - 0.34) + $60,000
   = $126,000

6. Asset with 5-year class life is fully-depreciated at end of year 6. Book value is equal to zero. Gain is equal to market value of $200,000.

   Taxes owed = ($200,000)(0.34) = $68,000

7. Purchase price $450,000
    Shipping charges   50,000
    Investment tax credit
      (8%)($500,000)   (40,000)
    Increase in net working capital
      ($15,000 - $8,000)   7,000
    Net investment cash outflow $467,000

8. Asset with a 5-year class life is fully-depreciated after 6 years. Depreciation equals zero for year 7.

   OCF = ($40,000)(1 - 0.40) = $24,000

9. Depreciation Schedule:

   Year 1 $125,000 × 0.3333 = $41,663
   Year 2 $125,000 × 0.4444 = $55,550
   Year 3 $125,000 × 0.1482 = $18,525

   Operating Cash Flows:

   Year 1 = ($60,000 - $10,000 - $41,663)(1 - 0.40) + $41,663 = $46,665
   Year 2 = ($60,000 - $10,000 - $55,550)(1 - 0.40) + $55,550 = $52,220
   Year 3 = ($60,000 - $10,000 - $18,525)(1 - 0.40) + $18,525 = $37,410

Chapter 8

10. Book value: $125,000 \times 0.0741 = \$9,263$
    Market value $\underline{\$9,000}$
    Loss $\$263$

    Tax savings = ($263)(0.40) = $105
    Net proceeds = $9,000 + $105 = $9,105

9 EVALUATING CAPITAL INVESTMENTS

OVERVIEW

Chapter 8 examined the generation of ideas for capital investments and the estimation of project cash flows. In this chapter, four methods available to financial managers for evaluating cash flows and selecting from among proposed projects are introduced. A discussion of potential conflict among the methodologies when projects are rank-ordered follows. Chapter 10 will present procedures for analyzing projects with differing levels of risk.

OUTLINE

When evaluating proposed capital projects, the evaluation method should ideally (1) include all cash flows occurring during the entire life of a project, (2) be consistent with the principle of time value of money, and (3) incorporate the required rate of return on the project.

- The merits of each of the four evaluation methods introduced in this chapter -- *payback period, net present value, profitability index* and *internal rate of return* -- will be considered using these criteria for an ideal evaluation method.

- To illustrate the application of each evaluation method, the following information on ABD Corp. will be used throughout the chapter outline:

    Net Investment Cash Outflow (NICO) = $12,000

Chapter 9

> Operating Cash Flows (OCF) = $3,500 per year for 7 years
> Disposal Cash Flow = $2,500 at end of year 7

The *payback period* is the time required to recover a project's net investment cash outflow (NICO) through incremental cash inflows.

- For ABD Corp., the payback period measures how many years it would take to recover the $12,000 NICO through the $3,500 annual operating cash flows. The first 3 years of OCF provide $10,500 (3 years × $3,500 per year), but an additional $1,500 is needed to recover NICO of $12,000. Year 4 provides another $3,500, but only $1,500 of that is needed. Assuming that cash flows occur uniformly throughout the year, it will take $1,500/$3,500 of year 4, or 0.43 of the year, to recover the $1,500.

  Payback period = 3 years + 0.43 year = 3.43 years

Once the payback period has been calculated, it must be compared to a standard set by the company to determine the project's acceptability.

- For example, if ABD's standard is 4 years or less, this project would be acceptable. If ABD's standard is 3 years or less, the project is not acceptable.

Payback period does not meet any of the criteria of an ideal evaluation method: (1) it does not consider cash flows that occur beyond the payback period; (2) the time value of money is not taken into account -- the annual cash flows of $3,500 were accorded equal weight even though those received earlier have higher present values than those received later; and (3) there is no consideration of the project's required rate of return.

- In fact, payback measures a return *of* invested capital rather than a return *on* invested capital. Because it does reflect a project's liquidity (speed of capital recovery), it is a popular evaluation method among financial managers whose companies are short of cash and operating in an uncertain environment. However, there are other methods available that better meet the criteria of an ideal evaluation method.

A project's *net present value (NPV)* is a dollar amount representing the present value of cash inflows minus the net investment cash outflow. The cash inflows are discounted using the required rate of return on the project, which for average-risk

projects is equal to the company's MCC.

- If ABD Corp.'s MCC is 20 percent, the net present value of this project would be:

$$\text{NPV} = \{(\$3,500)[1-(1.20)^{-7}]/0.20 + (\$2,500)(1.20)^{-7}]\} - \$12,000$$
$$= [(\$3,500)(3.6046) + (\$2,500)(0.2791)] - \$12,000$$
$$= (\$12,616 + \$698) - \$12,000$$
$$= \$13,314 - \$12,000$$
$$= \$1,314$$

Since net present value measures the dollar change in shareholder wealth, or dollar change in market value of common equity, a financial manager should accept any project with a positive net present value and reject any project with a negative net present value.

- The project ABD is considering has a positive NPV of $1,314 at a discount rate of 20 percent and should therefore be accepted. Project acceptance will increase stock price.

Net present value satisfies all criteria for an ideal evaluation method: (1) it uses all incremental cash flows; (2) it recognizes the time value of money; and (3) it incorporates the project's required rate of return.

The *profitability index (PI)* measures the present value of cash inflows per dollar of investment; PI is a benefit-cost ratio. The equations for net present value and the profitability index are closely related in that they use the same cash flows and discount rate. To calculate the profitability index, the present value of cash inflows is divided by the net investment cash outflow.

- For ABD Corp., the profitability index is:

$$\text{PI} = \$13,314/\$12,000 = 1.11$$

The company receives $1.11 in present value for each $1 invested.

The decision rule for the profitability index is as follows:

- PI > 1.0, accept the project. Stock price will rise.

Chapter 9

- PI < 1.0, reject the project. Acceptance would cause stock price to fall.

- PI = 1.0, acceptance or rejection would have no impact on stock price.

Since ABD's PI is greater than 1.0, the project should be accepted. Like the NPV, the profitability index method satisfies all criteria for an ideal evaluation procedure.

The *internal rate of return (IRR)* on a project is the company's rate of return on its invested capital. IRR is the discount rate that equates the present value of a project's expected cash inflows with its net investment cash outflow. Note that expected cash inflows for a project include all operating cash flows (OCF) and any project disposal cash flow.

- For ABD Corp., the IRR would be the discount rate that satisfies the following equation:

$$\$12,000 = \$3,500 \times [1-(1+IRR)^{-7}]/IRR + \$2,500 \times (1+IRR)^{-7}$$

ABD's NICO is $12,000. The OCF are $3,500 per year for 7 years; therefore, the annuity formula can be used to find the present value of the OCF. The $2,500 disposal cash flow is a single cash flow occurring at the end of year 7.

Solving for the IRR involves trying different discount rates until one is found that satisfies the equation. The present value interest factor tables may be used or the mathematical equations may be used to calculate the present value interest factors.

- For the ABD Corp. example, a discount rate of 20 percent, 7 periods, would yield the following:

$$(\$3,500)(3.6046) + (\$2,500)(0.2791) = \$13,314$$

This solution, $13,314, exceeds the NICO of $12,000. In order to get a *smaller* present value of cash inflows, a discount rate *greater* than 20 percent must be tried. At 25 percent, 7 periods:

$$(\$3,500)(3.1611) + (\$2,500)(0.2097) = \$11,588$$

Chapter 9

The 25 percent discount rate yields a present value that is less than the desired $12,000. Recall that the present value at 20 percent was greater than $12,000. Thus, the range has been narrowed to between 20 percent and 25 percent. The present value at 25 percent is very close to $12,000, but it may be possible to get even closer. To obtain a *larger* present value of cash inflows (closer to $12,000), a rate *lower* than 25 percent must be tried. Using a discount rate of 24 percent, 7 periods results in the following:

$$(\$3{,}500)(3.2423) + (\$2{,}500)(0.2218) = \$11{,}903$$

This solution is very close to matching the NICO of $12,000. To confirm that the IRR is approximately 24 percent, solve for the present value one more time using a discount rate of 23 percent. The present value of the cash flows equals $12,232 at 23 percent, 7 periods, confirming that the rate is somewhere between 23 percent and 24 percent. It is generally unnecessary to solve for an exact IRR. If an exact IRR is desired, a financial calculator may be used to arrive at one.

Once a project's internal rate of return has been determined, it is compared to the project's *hurdle rate*, a minimum rate of return required for accepting the project. For projects with average-risk, the company's marginal cost of capital (MCC) is the appropriate hurdle rate.

- If IRR > MCC, accept the project; stock price will rise.

- If IRR < MCC, reject the project; acceptance would cause stock price to fall.

- If IRR = MCC, its acceptance or rejection would have no impact on stock price.

    If ABD Corp.'s marginal cost of capital is 20 percent, this project would be acceptable since its IRR exceeds the MCC.

    Recall that the project's IRR was close to 24 percent -- *when the NPV is positive, the IRR will exceed the project's required rate of return, and stock price will rise upon acceptance.*

- When NPV is negative, the project's IRR is less than its required rate of return. Project acceptance will cause stock price to fall.

Chapter 9

- When NPV equals zero, the project's IRR is equal to its required rate of return, and project acceptance will have no impact on stock price.

The internal rate of return satisfies all criteria for an ideal capital-budgeting method: (1) it uses cash flows over the entire life of the project; (2) it adjusts cash flows for the time value of money; and (3) the decision rule for IRR incorporates the project's required rate of return.

- Some projects, because of the pattern and magnitude of their cash inflows and outflows, may have multiple IRRs. If that occurs, the IRRs should *not* be interpreted as returns on invested capital.

NPV, PI and IRR are considered discounted cash flow (DCF) methods because they incorporate the time value of money. Payback period is considered an undiscounted evaluation method because it does not incorporate the time value of money.

- Any conventional project that is acceptable using one of the DCF methods will be acceptable using either of the other two DCF methods.

Although the three DCF methods (NPV, PI, and IRR) provide consistent evaluations for accept-reject decisions, they may produce conflicting rank-orderings of projects. A financial manager may have to rank-order projects because they are mutually exclusive and/or because the company faces capital rationing.

- When projects are *mutually exclusive*, acceptance of one project precludes acceptance of another project. When projects are *independent* of each other, acceptance of one project does not affect acceptance or rejection of another project.

- Under *capital rationing*, a company has a limited supply of capital and cannot accept all projects with positive net present values.

- When projects must be ranked to select the better ones, the discounted cash flow methods sometimes conflict in the rankings they produce. For example, NPV may point to one project as superior but IRR may indicate that the other project should be selected.

To resolve conflicts in ranking, the financial manager should construct NPV profiles

Chapter 9

for the two projects.

- An *NPV profile* is a graph of NPV as a function of the discount rate. When conflict in ranking occurs, the two NPV profiles will cross at some discount rate called the *crossover rate*.

- If the discount rate used to calculate NPV is greater than the crossover rate, the NPV and IRR methods will rank the projects in the same order. This is called the *zone of ranking consistency*.

- If the discount rate used to calculate NPV is less than the crossover rate, NPV and IRR will rank projects in conflicting order. This is referred to as the *zone of ranking conflict*.

Resolution of the ranking conflict requires that the financial manager estimate a *reinvestment rate* and compare it with the crossover rate.

- The reinvestment rate is the rate of return the company expects to earn from investing a project's cash inflows.

- If the company can reinvest each project's cash flows at a rate greater than the crossover rate, the project with the higher *IRR* should be chosen.

- If the estimated reinvestment rate is less than the crossover rate, the project with the higher *NPV* should be selected.

In general, for companies facing severe capital rationing, there is a high probability that the reinvestment rate will be greater than the crossover rate, and therefore, the IRR should be used to rank projects.

- In the absence of capital rationing, where a company can invest in all profitable projects, there is a high likelihood that the reinvestment rate will be less than the crossover rate. NPV should be used to rank projects in this case.

The final step in capital budgeting is to monitor projects that have been accepted and evaluate projects that have been completed or abandoned.

Chapter 9

■ A *post-completion audit* is helpful in assessing the actual success or failure of projects so that the company can reward the managers involved in successful projects. The audit also aids the financial manager in improving the capital-budgeting process by uncovering weaknesses in the system.

GLOSSARY OF KEY TERMS

capital rationing: capital available to a company is limited; requires a company to forgo some projects with positive NPVs

crossover rate: discount rate that causes equality between net present values of projects; point where the NPV profiles intersect

discounted cash flow (DCF) methods: capital-budgeting methods that discount cash flows to account for the time value of money: internal rate of return, net present value, and profitability index

hurdle rate: minimum rate of return required for accepting a capital project; cutoff or screening rate for capital budgeting

internal rate of return (IRR): return on invested capital; discount rate that causes equality between the present value of cash inflows and the net investment cash outflow

mutually exclusive projects: dependency among projects wherein acceptance of one precludes acceptance of the other projects

net present value (NPV): present value of cash inflows less net investment cash outflow

NPV profile: graph of NPV as a function of the discount rate

payback period: time required to recover a project's net investment cash outflow through incremental cash inflows

post-completion audit: performance appraisal of a capital project to assess its success

profitability index (PI): present value of cash inflows per dollar of investment; benefit-cost ratio

reinvestment rate: rate of return a company can earn from investing a project's cash inflows

zone of ranking conflict: range of discount rates where net present value and internal rate of return rank projects differently

zone of ranking consistency: range of discount rates where net present value and internal rate of return rank projects identically

Chapter 9

MULTIPLE CHOICE SELF-TEST

1. The criteria for an ideal capital budgeting method are satisfied by all of the following except the

   a. payback period
   b. internal rate of return
   c. net present value
   d. profitability index
   e. all of the above satisfy the criteria

2. The time required to recover the net investment cash outflow in a project through the incremental cash inflows is the

   a. turnaround time
   b. break-even period
   c. payback period
   d. profitability index
   e. recovery period

3. Finding the IRR on a project is similar to finding the

   a. break-even level of cash inflows
   b. inflation-adjusted discount rate
   c. net present value of the cash inflows
   d. yield to maturity on a bond
   e. present value of the NICO

4. If a project's risk is similar to other average-risk projects of the company, the required rate of return on the project would be

   a. below the company's MCC
   b. below the risk-free rate
   c. equal to the company's MCC
   d. equal to the risk-free rate
   e. greater than the company's MCC

Chapter 9

5. When the acceptance of one project precludes the acceptance of another project, the projects are

   a. independent
   b. codependent
   c. mutually exclusive
   d. mutually inclusive
   e. unacceptable

6. An independent project should be accepted if

   a. the required rate of return is greater than its IRR
   b. the required rate of return is greater than the cost of capital
   c. the cost of capital is greater than the hurdle rate
   d. its IRR is greater than the hurdle rate
   e. the required rate of return is greater than the hurdle rate

7. If the NPV of a project is equal to zero when the discount rate is 10 percent, the IRR on the project is

   a. greater than 10 percent
   b. equal to 10 percent
   c. less than 10 percent
   d. equal to zero
   e. insufficient information given

8. If NICO for a project is $500,000 and the profitability index is 1.35, the NPV for the project is

   a. $135,000
   b. $175,000
   c. $370,370
   d. $500,000
   e. $675,000

Chapter 9

9. According to the profitability index, a project should be accepted when its

   a. PI < 0
   b. PI < 1.0
   c. PI = 1.0
   d. PI > 1.0
   e. none of the above

10. The internal rate of return and net present value methods always lead to the same accept/reject decision

    a. and either one can be used to evaluate independent projects
    b. but they can provide conflicting rankings because of the time disparity problem
    c. but they can provide conflicting rankings because of the size disparity problem
    d. but they can provide conflicting rankings for mutually exclusive projects
    e. all of the above are true

11. When rank-ordering projects, if the reinvestment rate is expected to be greater than the crossover rate, which of the following is true?

    a. IRR should be used to rank conflicting projects.
    b. NPV should be used to rank conflicting projects.
    c. PI should be used to rank conflicting projects.
    d. Payback period should be used to rank conflicting projects.
    e. none of the above

12. The final step in the capital budgeting process is the

    a. generation of ideas for projects
    b. post-completion audit
    c. project proposal
    d. distribution of profits
    e. reinvestment of cash flows

Chapter 9

PROBLEMS

1. Rolling Robotics, Inc. is considering the acquisition of electronic testing equipment having a 5-year life and a cost of $434,000. The equipment will be depreciated using MACRS and a 3-year class life. Net working capital of $67,300 will be invested when the company implements the project. Rolling Robotics' financial manager, Rob Rolling, estimates that the equipment can be sold for $75,000 and that the entire amount of net working capital can be recaptured when the company terminates the project. Sales attributable to the equipment are estimated at $365,000 for the first year and are expected to increase by 8 percent each year thereafter. Variable costs are estimated at 60 percent of sales. Fixed costs will total $50,000 per year. Rolling Robotics' cost of capital is 16 percent and its marginal tax rate is 34 percent. The maximum acceptable payback period on proposed projects is 4 years.

   a. *Calculate all incremental cash flows associated with this project.*

   b. *Calculate and interpret the project's payback period, net present value, profitability index, and internal rate of return.*

2. Cyclone Cycles is evaluating a new chain winder with a NICO of $100,000, annual operating cash inflows (after-tax) of $30,000 for 5 years, and a disposal cash flow of $25,000. Cyclone Cycles' requires a 10 percent rate of return on projects of this risk.

   Calculate the project's payback period, net present value, profitability index, and internal rate of return.

3. A financial manager must evaluate two proposed projects that are mutually exclusive, both having a hurdle rate of 12 percent. Project S (for Small) requires a net investment cash outflow of $30,000, and Project L (for Large) requires one of $60,000. The project cash flows are as follows:

	Project Cash Flows		
End of Year	0	1	2
Project S	-$30,000	0	+$46,875
Project L	-$60,000	0	+$86,400

Chapter 9

a. *Do NPV and IRR conflict in their ranking of the two projects?*

b. *Which project should the financial manager accept if the reinvestment rate is 10 percent?*

SOLUTIONS TO MULTIPLE CHOICE SELF-TEST

1. a   7. b
2. c   8. b
3. d   9. d
4. c   10. e
5. c   11. a
6. d   12. b

SOLUTIONS TO PROBLEMS

1. a. Incremental cash flows:

   1) Net Investment Cash Outflow

Purchase price	$434,000
Increase in net working capital	67,300
Net Investment Cash Outflow	$501,300

   2) Depreciation

      Year 1: ($434,000)(0.3333) = $144,652
      Year 2: ($434,000)(0.4444) = $192,870
      Year 3: ($434,000)(0.1482) = $ 64,319
      Year 4: ($434,000)(0.0741) = $ 32,159

Chapter 9

3) Operating Cash Flows

OCF_1 = ($365,000 - $219,000 - $50,000 - $144,652)(1 - 0.34) + $144,652
    = $112,542
OCF_2 = ($394,200 - $236,520 - $50,000 - $192,870)(1 - 0.34) + $192,870
    = $136,645
OCF_3 = ($425,736 - $255,442 - $50,000 - $64,319)(1 - 0.34) + $64,319
    = $101,263
OCF_4 = ($459,795 - $275,877 - $50,000 - $32,159)(1 - 0.34) + $32,159
    = $99,320
OCF_5 = ($496,579 - $297,947 - $50,000 - 0)(1 - 0.34) + 0
    = $98,097

4) Disposal Cash Flow

Sale of asset	$ 75,000
Taxes owed ($75,000)(0.34)	(25,500)
Recovery of net working capital	67,300
Disposal Cash Flow	$116,800

b. Evaluation of proposed project:

1) Payback Period

NICO = $501,300

OCF_1	$112,542
OCF_2	136,645
	$249,187
OCF_3	101,263
	$350,450
OCF_4	99,320
	$449,770

$501,300 - $449,770 = $51,530 to recover from OCF_5
    $51,530/$98,097 = 0.525
        Payback period = 4.525 years

Interpretation: Project's payback period exceeds company maximum of 4 years; therefore, project should be rejected.

2) Net Present Value

Year 1: $112,542(1.16)^{-1}$	$ 97,019
Year 2: $136,645(1.16)^{-2}$	101,549
Year 3: $101,263(1.16)^{-3}$	64,875
Year 4: $99,320(1.16)^{-4}$	54,854
Year 5: $(\$98,097 + \$116,800)(1.16)^{-5}$	102,315
Sum of PV of Cash Inflows	$420,612
Less Net Investment Cash Outflow	-501,300
Net Present Value	-$80,688

Interpretation: Project's NPV < 0; therefore, project should be rejected.

3) Profitability Index

PI = $420,612/$501,300 = 0.839

Interpretation: Project's PI < 1.0; therefore, project should be rejected.

4) Internal Rate of Return

IRR is discount rate that makes sum of PV of cash inflows equal to NICO, in this case $501,300. At a discount rate of 16%, the sum of the PV of cash inflows was $420,612. Therefore, a discount rate lower than 16% should be substituted to obtain a larger present value:

At 10%, sum of PV of cash inflows = $492,592
At 9%, sum of PV of cash inflows = $506,484
IRR is between 9% and 10%

Interpretation: IRR of 9-10% is less than the MCC of 16%; therefore, project should be rejected.

Chapter 9

2. Payback Period = $100,000/$30,000
   = 3.33 years

   NPV = {($30,000)[1-(1.10)$^{-5}$]/0.10 + ($25,000)(1.10)$^{-5}$]} - $100,000
   = [($30,000)(3.7908) + ($25,000)(0.6209)] - $100,000
   = ($113,724 + $15,523) - $100,000
   = $129,247 - $100,000
   = $29,247

   PI = $129,247/$100,000 = 1.29

   IRR: Since NPV is positive, IRR must be greater than the discount rate (10%).

   At 20%: ($30,000)(2.9906) + ($25,000)(0.4019)
   = $89,718 + $10,048
   = $99,766 (close to NICO of $100,000); therefore

   IRR is between 19% and 20%

3. a. To determine whether or not there is a conflict in rank order, calculate the NPV and IRR for each project:

	Net Present Value	Internal Rate of Return
Project S	$7,368	25%
Project L	$8,878	20%

   There is a conflict in ranking because Project S has a higher IRR but a lower NPV than Project L.

   b. To determine which project is preferable, calculate the crossover rate and compare it with the reinvestment rate.

   $$NPV_S = NPV_L$$
   ($46,875) × [1-(1+?)$^{-2}$]/? - $30,000 = ($86,400) × [1-(1+?)$^{-2}$]/? - $60,000
   $39,525 × [1-(1+?)$^{-2}$]/? = $30,000
   [1-(1+?)$^{-2}$]/? = 0.7590

Chapter 9

Appendix A.2 in the text shows that an interest factor of 0.7590 and an n of 2 are associated with an interest rate between 14% and 15%. The crossover rate is 14-15%, which is higher than the 10% reinvestment rate. When the reinvestment rate is less than the crossover rate, the financial manager should select the project with the higher net present value. In this case, the financial manager should select Project L.

Chapter 9

10

CAPITAL BUDGETING and RISK

OVERVIEW

In capital budgeting, financial managers frequently analyze proposed projects with risk levels that differ from the company average. This chapter examines how to determine if a proposed project's risk is different from the company average and how to analyze those projects that have different levels of risk. Measuring expected net present value and standard deviation of a distribution of possible NPVs is one approach to evaluating a project's risk. Other methods include scenario analysis, sensitivity analysis, and Monte Carlo simulation. Risk adjustments can be incorporated into the capital budgeting process through the use of risk-adjusted discount rates or certainty equivalent factors.

OUTLINE

From a capital budgeting perspective, risk is the uncertainty surrounding a project's net present value (NPV). The actual NPV may differ from the expected NPV because of unforeseen variation in the values of key inputs to the capital budgeting analysis. These variations may lead to either *cost overruns* **or** *cost underruns.*

- The net investment cash outflow (NICO) may be different than expected because (1) the cost of equipment, buildings, or land may change, (2) the U.S. Congress may change the corporate tax rate or reinstitute the investment tax credit, and (3) net working capital investment may be more or less than expected.

- Actual operating cash flows (OCF) may be different than expected because (1) there may be unforeseen changes in product prices, (2) demand for the output may be

Chapter 10

different than the forecast, (3) cost of goods sold may be higher or lower than anticipated, (4) selling and administrative expenses may deviate from expectations, and (5) income taxes and rules may change unexpectedly.

■ Disposal cash flow (DCF) associated with the termination of the project may differ from the expected amount because (1) disposal values of depreciable assets and current assets cannot be specified with certainty, and (2) the tax effect of gains or losses on disposal of assets may be different than expected.

■ The marginal cost of capital (MCC) could change as a result of (1) changes in the market required rate of return in response to monetary policy actions and changing economic conditions, and (2) changes in investors' perceptions of the risk associated with the company's investments.

One approach to evaluating a proposed project's risk is to construct a probability distribution of net present values using possible NPVs and their associated probabilities of occurrence. An expected net present value and a standard deviation can then be calculated.

■ The expected net present value ($\overline{NPV}$) is calculated as:

$$\overline{NPV} = P_1 NPV_1 + P_2 NPV_2 + \ldots P_n NPV_n$$
$$= \Sigma P_j NPV_j$$

where $\overline{NPV}$ equals the expected NPV, P_j equals probability of the possible net present value NPV_j, and n equals number of possible NPVs.

■ For example, Tasty Tortilla Factory is considering replacing its antiquated charcoal-fired tortilla oven with a new model. One oven under consideration is a conventional gas-fired model. The other choice is a newly designed solar-powered oven. Tasty has estimated the possible NPVs for both investments as follows:

Oven Type	Probability	Possible NPV
Gas	0.60	$40,000
	0.40	$15,000
Solar	0.70	$60,000
	0.30	-$10,000

Chapter 10

The possible NPVs and their associated probabilities constitute a *discrete probability distribution*. There are a limited number of possible NPVs, each with its own probability. Gaps exist between the possible NPVs.:

The expected net present values of the ovens are:

$$\overline{NPV}_{gas} = 0.60(\$40,000) + 0.40(\$15,000)$$
$$= \$30,000$$

$$\overline{NPV}_{solar} = 0.70(\$60,000) + 0.30(-\$10,000)$$
$$= \$39,000$$

The solar-powered oven has a higher $\overline{NPV}$ than the gas-fired oven, but it would be premature to make a selection between the two ovens without first measuring their risk. Preference for a project depends not only on the size of the expected NPV but also on its risk.

■ The standard deviation (σ) quantifies risk by measuring the dispersion of a distribution of net present values:

■ For Tasty Tortilla Factory, the standard deviations of the two projects under consideration are:

$$\sigma = \sqrt{\Sigma P(NPV - \overline{NPV})^2}$$

$$\sigma_{gas} = \sqrt{0.60(\$40,000 - \$30,000)^2 + 0.40(\$15,000 - \$30,000)^2}$$

$$= \sqrt{\$60,000,000 + \$90,000,000}$$

$$= \sqrt{\$150,000,000}$$

$$= \$12,247$$

Chapter 10

$$\sigma_{solar} = \sqrt{0.70(\$60{,}000 - \$39{,}000)^2 + 0.30(\$10{,}000 - \$39{,}000)^2}$$

$$= \sqrt{\$308{,}700{,}000 + \$720{,}300{,}000}$$

$$= \sqrt{\$1{,}029{,}000{,}000}$$

$$= \$32{,}078$$

The solar-powered oven's larger standard deviation reflects a wider dispersion of possible outcomes and a greater chance that the actual NPV will differ from the expected. The solar-powered oven involves greater risk.

Three alternative methods for assessing the risk of a capital project are *scenario analysis*, *sensitivity analysis*, and *Monte Carlo simulation*.

- In *scenario analysis*, a project is analyzed under three different sets of assumptions: (1) the most likely case, (2) a pessimistic (worst) case, and (3) an optimistic (best) case. For example, under the worst case scenario, the financial manager might use an inflated cash outflow, reduced cash inflows, a shortened project life, and a higher discount rate, all factors leading to a lower net present value. The best case scenario would contain optimistic estimates of the different variables. The final decision still depends on intuition and judgment rather than a universal accept-reject decision rule, but scenario analysis forces the financial manager to consider the possibility of variables gone awry and to plan for contingencies.

- *Sensitivity analysis* measures the impact of changes in inputs, taken one at a time, on a project's net present value (or its internal rate of return or profitability index). It can be thought of as a *what if* analysis -- what happens to NPV if one variable changes by a certain percentage? A wide variety of different inputs can be evaluated: estimated project lives, cash inflows, operating costs, number of units sold, price per unit sold, and changes in tax laws. Sensitivity analysis allows identification of the variables with the greatest impact on NPV.

- *Monte Carlo simulation* develops a probability distribution of net present values using probability distributions of key input variables. Values are randomly selected from the distributions for each input variable and combined to calculate net present value. This process is repeated a large number of times (for example, 1000) to generate a distribution of NPVs for a project. For many capital projects, Monte Carlo simulation produces NPV distributions that are near normal, allowing financial managers to make probability statements about NPV.

One method available to financial managers for incorporating risk in the capital budgeting process is the *risk-adjusted discount rate (RADR)*. The basic premise is that higher risk projects should be evaluated using a higher discount rate than lower risk projects.

- The marginal cost of capital (MCC) is used to evaluate projects with typical or average risk. MCC, the weighted average of the component costs of capital, reflects investors' perceptions about the risk of company assets as a whole. Therefore, projects having risk similar to that of the company are evaluated at a required rate of return equal to the MCC.

- Projects that have greater risk than the company's average asset should be evaluated with a discount rate that exceeds the MCC. A discount rate lower than the MCC should be used for projects that have less risk than the company's average. These risk-adjusted discount rates can be used in calculating the project's net present value and profitability index or in evaluating a project's internal rate of return.

- Some financial managers establish risk classes for capital projects, assigning each class a specified discount rate. Other financial managers prefer to use the *pure-play method*, where the risk-adjusted discount rate for a proposed project is estimated using the MCC of a publicly held company in the same line of business as the proposed project. However, pure-play companies are often difficult to identify because so many companies have diverse operations.

An alternative to risk-adjusted discount rates is the use of *certainty equivalents*. Instead of adjusting the discount rate for risk, certainty equivalents adjust a project's risky *cash flows* to make them equal in desirability to risk-free cash flows.

- The relationship between a certain cash inflow and a risky cash inflow is:

    Certain cash flow = α_t × Risky cash flow

Chapter 10

where α is the certainty equivalent factor for the risky cash flow occurring at time t. These factors range between zero and 1.0 for risky cash inflows. For risky cash outflows, the factors exceed 1.0. Cash inflows are reduced in size to compensate for risk; cash outflows are increased in size to compensate for risk.

Note that certainty equivalent factors for cash inflows normally decline over time, reflecting increasing uncertainty about the more distant cash inflows.

- Once the cash flows have been adjusted for risk using α, the *risk-free rate of return*, R_f, is used to calculate the present values of the certainty equivalent cash flows. The risk-free rate is used as the discount rate because the expected cash flows have already been adjusted for risk. The normal decision rules hold for accepting-rejecting projects under this method.

The capital asset pricing model (CAPM) can be used in capital budgeting for capital projects that trade in markets similar to those for common stocks and for projects with securities that trade. According to the CAPM, only the nondiversifiable portion of project risk should be used to adjust the discount rate.

- The CAPM describes the required rate of return on a project as:

$$K = R_f + (K_m - R_f)\beta$$

where β measures the *project's* nondiversifiable risk. If the expected internal rate of return on a proposed projects exceeds the required rate of return (K), the project should be accepted. The required rate of return given by the CAPM can also be used to calculate the project's net present value or profitability index.

- The application of the CAPM in capital budgeting is limited by the fact that most capital projects do not trade in markets and most projects do not have securities that trade. An exception would be the purchase of a subsidiary or an entire company whose securities actively trade in the securities market. Another drawback to using the CAPM is the difficulty in estimating project betas.

The concept of risk, its measurement, and its impact on stock price are all too elusive for reliance solely on the validity of any one method for addressing risk.

Chapter 10

■ Financial managers would be wise to use a combination of the evaluation methods discussed in this chapter to assess a project's risk and incorporate that risk into the capital budgeting process. Ultimately, the financial manager's intuition and judgment will be integral to making sound decisions regarding capital investments. There are no easy answers to the hard questions posed by project risk.

GLOSSARY OF KEY TERMS

certainty equivalent adjustment (CEA): adjustment to a risky cash flow making it equally desirable to a risk-free cash flow; technique for analyzing risky capital investments

discrete probability distribution: probability distribution comprising a limited number of outcomes and their associated probabilities

Monte Carlo simulation: method for producing a probability distribution of NPVs based on probability distributions of key input variables

pure-play method: technique for estimating the required rate of return on a proposed investment; use the estimated MCC of a publicly held company in the same line of business as the proposed project

risk-adjusted discount rate (RADR): rate of return adjusted for the uncertainty in future cash flows; technique for analyzing risky capital investments

scenario analysis: analysis of a capital project's acceptability under three sets of assumptions: pessimistic, most likely, and optimistic

sensitivity analysis: analysis of the effects that key input variables, changed one at a time, have on the acceptability of a capital project

Chapter 10

MULTIPLE CHOICE SELF-TEST

1. Risk in a capital project may result from variations in

   a. the net investment cash outflow
   b. operating cash flows
   c. the disposal cash flow
   d. the marginal cost of capital
   e. all of the above

2. Which of the following leads to uncertainty in capital budgeting?

   a. the actual NICO is less than expected because Congress reinstates the investment tax credit
   b. the actual MCC is lower than the expected MCC
   c. the actual disposal cash flow is greater than expected because the resale price of the asset turns out to be higher than anticipated
   d. the actual operating cash flows are lower than expected because the cost savings are less than anticipated
   e. all of the above are examples of risk

3. The expected net present value is calculated as

   a. a probability-weighted average of possible NPVs
   b. the median of a continuous probability distribution
   c. the best guess estimate
   d. the value that causes IRR to equal the hurdle rate
   e. zero

4. Capital projects A and B both have expected NPVs of $100,000. The standard deviation of A's NPV equals $10,000; B's standard deviation equals $15,000.

   a. Both A and B are risk free.
   b. A is riskier than B.
   c. A and B are equally risky.
   d. B is riskier than A.
   e. Both A and B are too risky.

Chapter 10

5. Analyzing projects under three different sets of assumptions is

   a. scenario analysis
   b. not of value
   c. sensitivity analysis
   d. redundancy testing
   e. simulation analysis

6. The variables with the greatest impact on NPV are identified with

   a. an extensive search
   b. sensitivity analysis
   c. percentage analysis
   d. simulation analysis
   e. a bloodhound

7. The method for producing a probability distribution of NPVs based on probability distributions of key input variables is called

   a. certainty equivalence factors
   b. pure-play method
   c. scenario analysis
   d. Monte Carlo simulation
   e. sensitivity analysis

8. The appropriate discount rate to use when calculating a certainty equivalent NPV is the

   a. risk-free rate
   b. company's MCC
   c. expected return on the market portfolio
   d. project's hurdle rate
   e. required rate of return on common equity

Chapter 10

9. One difficulty in applying the CAPM to capital budgeting decisions is

   a. it does not permit the calculation of multiple hurdle rates
   b. it cannot be used for an all-equity firm
   c. the betas of projects are not easily measured
   d. it cannot be used for an NPV calculation
   e. a proxy for the risk-free rate of return is not readily available

10. Which of the following statements about Monte Carlo simulation is not true?

    a. It requires that a financial manager develop probability distributions for investment cost, market conditions, operating costs, selling price, economic life, and disposal value.
    b. It utilizes a computer program to randomly select values from each probability distribution.
    c. It calculates many value for NPV.
    d. It calculates expected NPV and the standard deviation of NPV.
    e. all of the above are true

Chapter 10

PROBLEMS

Use the following information for problems 1 to 4:

Blues Brothers, Inc. (BBI) is considering a capital investment proposal for the next year. The project requires a $35,000 net investment cash outflow and has the following cash inflows:

Scenario	Year 1	Year 2	Year 3
Optimistic	$20,000	$26,000	$16,000
Most likely	$16,000	$20,000	$10,000
Pessimistic	$10,000	$12,000	$ 4,000

BBI's financial manager estimates the marginal cost of capital for the company to be 16 percent. The risk-free rate of return is estimated at 8 percent.

1. Assuming the proposed project is of average risk to BBI, calculate its net present value under each scenario.

2. The financial manager believes that the probability of the optimistic scenario occurring is 15 percent, and assigns a 70 percent probability for the most likely scenario. Based on this, what is the expected net present value of the project?

3. Now assume that the project is of greater-than-average risk. According to company guidelines, projects with risk characteristics such as this one require a minimum expected return premium of 2 percentage points over the company's marginal cost of capital. Calculate the net present value for the most likely scenario based on this risk-adjusted rate.

Chapter 10

4. The financial manager decides to compare the above results with an analysis using certainty equivalent adjustments. Based on risk levels of the likely cash flows, the following certainty equivalent factors are used:

Cash Flow	Certainty Equivalent Factor
Year 1	0.98
Year 2	0.92
Year 3	0.85

   Calculate the net present value of the project for the most likely scenario based on this information.

   Use the following information for problems 5 through 8:

   Lisa has inherited $100,000 from her aunt Lucille and has decided to invest it in a new laundromat-cafe called the Wash n' Dine. Lisa estimated NPVs from the project as $50,000 with a probability of 60 percent and -$30,000 with a probability of 40 percent.

5. Calculate the expected NPV of the Wash n' Dine project.

6. Calculate the standard deviation of the proposed project.

7. Lisa has estimated the beta for the Wash n' Dine at 1.5. The expected return on the market portfolio is 12 percent and the risk-free rate is 6 percent. What is the required rate of return for the project?

8. The risky operating cash inflows for Wash n' Dine have been estimated at $35,200 per year for five years, and the certainty equivalent factor is 0.74 for each cash flow. Calculate the certainty equivalent NPV for the project.

9. To increase production, Tempered Tiles, Inc. is considering an investment in new manufacturing equipment having a NICO of $600,000. The company is all equity financed and the new equipment will be bought with retained earnings. With a beta of 1.75, common stock in Tempered Tiles has a required rate of return of 15

percent, and the risk-free rate is 8 percent. The project cash inflows for the new equipment have been estimated under three different scenarios as follows:

Scenario	Probability	Year 1	Year 2	Year 3
Optimistic	0.25	$300,000	$325,000	$350,000
Most likely	0.45	$250,000	$250,000	$250,000
Pessimistic	0.30	$150,000	$160,000	$170,000

If the project is of average risk to Tempered Tiles and the expected disposal cash flow at the end of the third year is $100,000, what is the NPV for the most likely scenario?

10. BLT Company has a beta of 1.4 and a marginal cost of capital of 20 percent. It is considering expansion into a related line of business, for which the pure-play beta is 1.8. Assuming the risk-free rate of return is 6 percent, find the required risk-adjusted rate of return for the project.

SOLUTIONS TO MULTIPLE CHOICE SELF-TEST

1. e   6. b
2. e   7. d
3. a   8. a
4. d   9. c
5. a   10. e

Chapter 10

SOLUTIONS TO PROBLEMS

1. For each scenario:

   NPV = [(Year 1 CF)$(1.16)^{-1}$ + (Year 2 CF)$(1.16)^{-2}$
   + (Year 3 CF)$(1.16)^{-3}$] - $35,000

   PVIF at 16%: Year 1 = 0.8621; Year 2 = 0.7432; Year 3 = 0.6407

   Optimistic:
   NPV = [($20,000)(0.8621) + ($26,000)(0.7432)
   + ($16,000)(0.6407)] - $35,000
   = ($17,242 + $19,323 + $10,251) - $35,000
   = $46,816 - $35,000
   = $11,816

   Most Likely:
   NPV = [($16,000)(0.8621) + ($20,000)(0.7432)
   + ($10,000)(0.6407)] - $35,000
   = ($13,794 + $14,864 + $6,407) - $35,000
   = $35,065 - $35,000
   = $65

   Pessimistic:
   NPV = [($10,000)(0.8621) + ($12,000)(0.7432)
   + ($4,000)(0.6407)] - $35,000
   = ($8,621 + $8,918 + $2,563) - $35,000
   = $20,102 - $35,000
   = -$14,898

2. The expected net present value is a probability-weighted average of possible NPVs:

    Expected NPV = 0.15($11,816) + 0.70($65) + 0.15(-$14,898)
     = $1,772 + $46 + -$2,235
     = -$417

3. K = 16% + 2% = 18%

    PVIF at 18%: Year 1 = 0.8475; Year 2 = 0.7182; Year 3 = 0.6086

    Most Likely:
    NPV = [($16,000)(0.8475) + ($20,000)(0.7182)
     + ($10,000)(0.6086)] - $35,000
     = ($13,560 + $14,364 + $6,086) - $35,000
     = $34,010 - $35,000
     = -$990

4. Most Likely:
    Year 1 = 0.98($16,000) = $15,680
    Year 2 = 0.92($20,000) = $18,400
    Year 3 = 0.85($10,000) = $8,500

    K = 8% (use risk-free rate with certainty equivalents)
    PVIF at 8%: Year 1 = 0.9259; Year 2 = 0.8573; Year 3 = 0.7938

    NPV = [($15,680)(0.9259) + ($18,400)(0.8573)
     + ($8,500)(0.7938)] - $35,000
     = ($14,518 + $15,774 + $6,747) - $35,000
     = $37,039 - $35,000
     = $2,039

5. Expected NPV = 0.6($50,000) + 0.4(-$30,000)
     = $30,000 + -$12,000
     = $18,000

Chapter 10

6. Variance = $0.6(\$50,000 - \$18,000)^2$
   $+ 0.4(-\$30,000 - \$18,000)^2$
   = $\$614,400,000 + \$921,600,000$
   = $\$1,536,000,000$

   The standard deviation equals the square root of the variance, or $39,192.

7. K = 6% + (12% - 6%)(1.5)
   = 6% + 9%
   = 15%

8. Certainty equivalent cash inflows = 0.74($35,200) = $26,048

   K = 6% (use risk-free rate with certainty equivalents)
   PVIFA at 6%, 5 years = 4.2124

   NPV = ($26,048)(4.2124) - $100,000
   = $109,725 - $100,000
   = $9,725

9. Most Likely:

   PVIFA 15%, 3 years = 2.2832; PVIF 15%, 3 years = 0.6575

   NPV = [($250,000)(2.2832) + ($100,000)(0.6575)] - $600,000
   = ($570,800 + $65,750) - $600,000
   = $636,550 - $600,000
   = $36,550

10. 20% = 6% + (Market price of risk)(1.4)
    14% = 1.4(Market price of risk)
    10% = Market price of risk

Required return on project:

$$K = 6\% + (10\%)(1.8)$$
$$= 6\% + 18\%$$
$$= 24\%$$

Chapter 10

11 WORKING CAPITAL POLICIES

OVERVIEW

Working-capital management is the management of all components of a company's current assets and current liabilities. This chapter describes the principles of working-capital management and points out trade-offs faced by financial managers: (1) liquidity versus expected profitability and (2) aggressive versus conservative financing of current assets. The chapter also presents a statement of cash flows, which shows the change in a company's cash balance due to operating, investing, and financing activities.

OUTLINE

The *liquidity* of an asset is the ease with which it can be converted into cash at the prevailing market value without large transaction costs. *Company liquidity*, the ability to meet short-term financial obligations, increases with the level of investment in liquid assets (cash, T-bills, and other marketable securities).

- Liquidity has both benefits and costs for a company. Liquid assets increase the company's ability to take advantage of business opportunities, such as discounts offered by suppliers for prompt payment of bills. Liquidity also shields a company against unexpected problems and thus lessens default risk, the risk of being unable to repay maturing debts.

- However, holding liquid assets generates both opportunity costs and out-of-pocket

179

costs. For example, holding cash, instead of investing it elsewhere to earn a return, creates an opportunity cost for a company. Holding inventory for sale involves the payment of storage fees, insurance, taxes, and other out-of-pocket expenses.

The costs and benefits of holding liquid assets result in a trade-off between a company's *liquidity* and its *expected profitability*.

- Liquidity and profitability are inversely related: An increase in liquidity causes a decrease in expected profitability, and a decrease in liquidity causes an increase in expected profitability.

A company's balance sheet can be interpreted as a trade-off between liquidity and expected profitability.

- Assets are listed according to decreasing liquidity and increasing expected profitability. Thus, cash, the most liquid but least profitable asset, is listed first. Fixed assets, which are less liquid but generate more profit for the company, are listed last.

- Liabilities and equity are listed in order of increasing liquidity and decreasing expected profitability. Current liabilities (listed first) represent a near-term cash need, which is a decrease of a company's liquidity. However, current liabilities normally have no or low interest costs compared to longer-term liabilities and are therefore more profitable. Long-term debt and equity (listed last) increase company liquidity by reducing near-term cash needs, but the cost of long-term financing usually exceeds that of short-term financing, resulting in lower expected profitability.

Measures of liquidity included in this chapter are current ratio, net working capital, and current asset turnover. Expected profitability, which can be measured by many different ratios, is measured by return on assets.

$$\text{Current ratio} = \text{Current assets}/\text{Current liabilities}$$

- A large current ratio means the company has the potential to pay current liabilities by liquidating current assets. A current ratio of less than 1.0 would indicate low liquidity -- the company would not have enough current assets to cover current liabilities.

$$\text{Net working capital} = \text{Current assets} - \text{Current Liabilities}$$

Chapter 11

A large amount of net working capital indicates that current assets easily cover current liabilities. Positive net working capital can also be viewed as the portion of current assets financed with long-term debt and equity, since it is the amount over and above current liabilities.

Current asset turnover = Sales/Current assets

Current asset turnover measures the extent to which a company works it current assets -- the number of dollars of sales generated per dollar of current assets. A large current asset turnover ratio indicates that the company is generating more sales dollars for each dollar of current assets; it is working its current assets harder.

Return on assets (ROA) = Earnings after taxes/Total assets

Return on assets is one measure of a company's expected profitability. The higher the ROA, the more profitable the company's operations.

Working-capital policy **consists of a set of rules describing the way a company deals with the dilemma arising from the trade-off between liquidity and expected profitability. The two extremes in working-capital policy are described as** *conservative* **or** *aggressive.*

■ A conservative working-capital policy emphasizes liquidity at the expense of profitability. An aggressive working-capital policy emphasizes expected profitability at the expense of liquidity.

A company with a conservative working-capital policy would have the following characteristics:

> High level of current assets
> Low level of current liabilities
> High current ratio
> Large amount of net working capital
> Low current asset turnover
> High expected sales
> Low expected return on assets

Chapter 11

- The company's high level of current assets may lead to high sales as the result of a liberal credit policy and an extensive inventory. The high level of current assets has a cost, though -- bad-debt expense may be high due to the company's liberal credit policy and inventory holding costs may also be high. These costs, combined with the use of more expensive long-term financing, cause expected profitability to be lower.

A company with an aggressive working-capital policy would have the following characteristics:

> Low level of current assets
> High level of current liabilities
> Low current ratio
> Small amount of net working capital
> High current asset turnover
> Low expected sales
> High expected return on assets

- Low expected sales may result from a very tight (stringent) credit policy and a low level of inventory. The company may lose sales to customers who are denied credit or who cannot find the product they need because of stockouts. Despite the lost sales, expected profitability may increase because of reduced bad-debt expense, reduced storage costs for inventory, and interest savings on long-term debt.

The *matching principle* advises managers to match the maturity of capital sources with the maturity of their uses.

- Application of this principle requires a distinction between two different types of current assets. *Permanent current assets* form a base level of total current assets that does not change from season to season. They represent a minimum level of cash, receivables, and inventory that a company must maintain to stay in business. *Temporary current assets*, on the other hand, are the part of total current assets that fluctuate with seasonal demand.

According to the matching principle, all permanent assets should be financed with long-term financing. This means both fixed assets and permanent current assets should be financed with long-term debt and equity. Temporary current assets should

be financed with current liabilities.

Some financial managers choose to violate the matching principle.

- Managers employing a conservative working-capital policy may finance not only fixed assets and permanent current assets but also some *temporary* current assets with long-term financing. The objective is to increase liquidity by using more long-term financing, but the policy may result in excess working capital during the low points of temporary current assets. Because of the excess working capital and the higher cost of long-term capital, the conservative policy lessens the company's expected profitability.

- Managers employing an aggressive working-capital policy may use current liabilities to finance not only temporary current assets but also part of the *permanent* current assets. The objective is to increase profitability by using cheaper short-term financing, but the policy exposes the company to *refinancing risk*. Refinancing risk is the possibility of not being able to refinance the short-term debt when it matures, or having to refinance it at a higher-than-expected interest rate.

A *statement of cash flows* shows the financial manager the details of past activities causing a change in the company's cash balance. The statement classifies company activities into three categories:

- *Operating activities*: Producing and delivering goods and services. Includes earnings after taxes plus depreciation and cash flows from changes in current assets and current liabilities.

- *Investing activities*: Acquiring and selling fixed assets, lending money, receiving loan repayments, and acquiring and selling marketable securities other than cash equivalents. (Cash equivalents mature in 90 days or less.)

- *Financing activities*: Obtaining cash from owners and creditors, paying dividends, repurchasing stock, and retiring debt.

The first step in preparing a statement of cash flows is to compare beginning and ending balances of balance sheet accounts (other than cash) to determine the impact of any account changes on cash.

Chapter 11

- The following rule is useful in identifying increases and decreases in cash:

Increases in Cash	Decreases in Cash
Decrease in assets	Increases in assets
Increase in liabilities	Decreases in liabilities

    Each balance sheet account change is listed as an increase in cash or a decrease in cash based on this classification.

    The increases and decreases in cash are then rearranged to group together the changes attributable to operating, investing, and financing activities. Earnings after taxes (from the income statement) is included under operating activities.

- Combining the cash flows produced by operating, investing, and financing activities yields an increase or decrease in cash for the period. The change in cash is the balancing item of the statement of cash flows.

A financial manager uses a statement of cash flows for three purposes:

- To assess the impact of operations on the company's cash balance.

- To evaluate the flow of cash from activities other than operations.

- To determine how the company used cash during the period.

   Comparing statements for several periods enables managers to discern important developing trends.

GLOSSARY OF KEY TERMS

aggressive working-capital policy: policy that emphasizes profitability over liquidity
conservative working-capital policy: policy that emphasizes liquidity over profitability
current asset turnover: sales per dollar of current assets
current ratio: investment in current assets per dollar of current liabilities; measure of a company's liquidity
liquidity: ease with which an asset can be converted into cash at the prevailing market value without large transaction costs
matching principle: matching the maturity of capital sources with the maturity of their uses
net working capital: current assets minus current liabilities; dollar amount of current assets financed with long-term debt and equity
permanent current assets: base level of current assets over an operating cycle
refinancing risk: possibility of not being able to refinance short-term debt when it matures; or the possibility of higher interest rates upon refinancing
return on assets (ROA): earnings after taxes per dollar of total assets; measure of a company's profitability
statement of cash flows: statement detailing changes in cash during a past operating period
temporary current assets: part of current assets that changes with seasonal demand
working-capital policy: company policy regarding the management of current assets and current liabilities

Chapter 11

MULTIPLE CHOICE SELF-TEST

1. Working-capital management is directly concerned with all of the following except

    a. inventory
    b. accounts payable
    c. short-term securities
    d. fixed assets
    e. taxes payable

2. The most liquid asset held by a company is

    a. common stock
    b. inventory
    c. retained earnings
    d. accounts receivable
    e. cash

3. A reduction in the level of liquidity would normally lead to

    a. increased expected profitability
    b. increased long-term liabilities
    c. decreased expected profitability
    d. decreased current liabilities
    e. financial distress

Chapter 11

4. Which of the following statements is true?

   a. A large current ratio implies that a company has very little net working capital.
   b. When net working capital is positive, the current ratio is less than 1.0.
   c. Net working capital is equal to current assets divided by current liabilities.
   d. Net working capital is the dollar amount of current assets financed with long-term debt and equity.
   e. A company with an aggressive working-capital policy has more net working capital than a similar company employing a conservative working-capital policy.

5. The extent to which a company works its current assets is measured by its

   a. current ratio
   b. current asset turnover
   c. net working capital
   d. return on assets
   e. temporary current assets

6. An aggressive financial manager attempts to operate with

   a. a minimum amount of current assets
   b. a large amount of long-term debt
   c. a low level of profitability
   d. maximum total assets
   e. a minimum amount of current liabilities

7. Which of the following is not characteristic of a firm practicing conservative working-capital management?

   a. high level of current assets
   b. high level of current liabilities
   c. low current asset turnover
   d. high expected sales
   e. low expected return on assets

Chapter 11

8. The appropriate level of working capital investment is the amount that is expected to

   a. maximize return on total assets
   b. maximize earnings per share
   c. maximize shareholder wealth
   d. minimize interest expense
   e. none of the above

9. A company that uses solely short-term financing to finance fluctuating, or temporary, current assets is employing which of the following practices?

   a. conservative
   b. matching
   c. aggressive
   d. moderate
   e. none of the above

10. Which of the following does not change with seasonal changes in demand?

    a. temporary current assets
    b. permanent current assets
    c. total current assets
    d. total assets
    e. all of the above change with seasonal changes in demand

11. With the matching principle approach to meeting the financing needs of the firm, fixed and permanent current assets are financed with

    a. long-term debt
    b. short-term debt
    c. equity
    d. a and c
    e. none of the above

12. Preparing a statement of cash flows requires calculating the dollar change in

    a. current assets
    b. current liabilities
    c. long-term debt
    d. fixed assets
    e. all of the above

13. Which of the following is not a classification of company activities normally found on a statement of cash flows?

    a. investing
    b. financing
    c. distributing
    d. operating
    e. all of the above are normally found

14. Which of the following transactions represents an increase in cash on a company's statement of cash flows?

    a. payment of dividends to shareholders
    b. paying off accounts payable
    c. retirement of long-term debt
    d. granting trade credit
    e. charging purchases

Chapter 11

PROBLEMS

Use the following information for Problems 1, 2, and 3:

Bob's Backhoe and Logging Company (BackLog) has current assets of $630,000, current liabilities of $450,000, and annual sales of $2,600,000.

1. Calculate BackLog's net working capital.

2. Calculate BackLog's current ratio.

3. Calculate Backlog's current asset turnover.

4. The PDQ Corp. showed the following balances on its year-end balance sheets:

	1997	1998
Cash	$360,000	$?
Accounts receivable	180,000	225,000
Inventory	270,000	252,000
Fixed assets (gross)	630,000	630,000
Accumulated depreciation	225,000	252,000
Accounts payable	450,000	414,000
Taxes payable	90,000	72,000
Long-term debt	450,000	621,000
Shareholders' equity	225,000	288,000

What is the total of all increases in cash for the period shown? What is the total of all decreases in cash for the period shown? What number should appear as the cash balance in the 1998 column?

Chapter 11

Use the following information for Problems 5 and 6:

Mr. Chips Cookie Company has the following balance sheet as of December 31, 1997:

Assets		Liabilities and Equity	
Cash	$ 5,000	Accounts payable	$ 20,000
Receivables	25,000	Notes payable	15,000
Inventory	50,000	Long-term debt	30,000
Fixed assets	100,000	Shareholder equity	115,000
Total	$180,000	Total	$180,000

Mr. Chips had sales in 1997 of $350,000.

5. Calculate the net working capital, current ratio, and current asset turnover for Mr. Chips.

6. Compare Mr. Chips' liquidity level with the industry average. Companies in the cookie business have an average current ratio of 1.2 and an average current asset turnover of 5.0.

SOLUTIONS TO MULTIPLE CHOICE SELF-TEST

1. d
2. e
3. a
4. d
5. b
6. a
7. b
8. c
9. b
10. b
11. d
12. e
13. c
14. e

Chapter 11

SOLUTIONS TO PROBLEMS

1. Net working capital = $630,000 - $450,000
   = $180,000

2. Current ratio = $630,000/$450,000
   = 1.4

3. Current asset turnover = $2,600,000/$630,000
   = 4.13

4.

	Increase	Decrease
Accounts receivable		$45,000
Inventory	$ 18,000	
Fixed assets (gross)	0	0
Accumulated depreciation	27,000	
Accounts payable		36,000
Taxes payable		18,000
Long-term debt	171,000	
Shareholders' equity	63,000	
Total	$279,000	$99,000

   Net cash increase = $279,000 - $99,000 = $180,000
   Cash balance = $360,000 + $180,000 = $540,000

5. Current assets = $5,000 + $25,000 + $50,000
   = $80,000
   Current liabilities = $20,000 + $15,000
   = $35,000
   Net working capital = $80,000 - $35,000
   = $45,000
   Current ratio = $80,000/$35,000
   = 2.3
   Current asset turnover = $350,000/$80,000
   = 4.38

6. Company liquidity is substantially higher than the industry average, suggesting that Mr. Chips should have no problems in meeting its short-term payment obligations. The high degree of liquidity suggests that the company is following a conservative working-capital policy. Conservatism is also reflected in the company's relatively low current asset turnover.

Chapter 11

12 WORKING CAPITAL PRACTICES

OVERVIEW

Working capital practices entail managing both current assets and current liabilities. This chapter discusses the techniques and practices financial managers use to manage cash, accounts receivable, inventory and current liabilities. Working capital practices involve managing the trade-off between liquidity and profitability.

OUTLINE

Companies hold cash because the timing and amount of cash inflows do not match the timing and amount of cash outflows. The holding of cash subjects companies to purchasing-power risk and opportunity cost.

- Purchasing-power risk is the uncertainty about how much future purchasing-power today's money will have. Holding cash during periods of inflation subjects a company to a purchasing-power loss.

- The opportunity cost of holding cash relates to the fact that many companies hold cash in non-interest-bearing checking accounts. The opportunity cost is the interest that could have been earned if the cash had been invested.

The cash balance of a company can be viewed as consisting of five parts.

- A *transactions balance* represents cash held because receipts and expenditures are not perfectly synchronized. It acts as a buffer between unmatched cash inflows and outflows.

- A *precautionary balance* is held to guard against unexpected losses or emergencies that may occur and cause greater cash outflows than anticipated.

- A *speculative balance* may be held in order to have cash to take advantage of unexpected investment opportunities. Speculative balances are often held in marketable securities, where interest may be earned, until they are invested elsewhere.

- A *planning balance* represents cash held for expected capital expenditures. The cash often comes from retained earnings earmarked for future investment or from the proceeds of a new securities issue.

- A *compensating balance* is cash deposited in a commercial bank account as a condition for obtaining a bank loan or service.

  The company's overall cash balance is not merely a sum of all the cash balances described. Some balances may serve more than one purpose.

In the study of cash management, it is important to understand the distinction between cash flow and earnings.

- Earnings are affected by *noncash* transactions such as credit sales, credit purchases, and depreciation expense. Cash flow can be affected by transactions that may not be reflected in earnings, such as the payment of dividends or the issuance of new securities.

- The following are examples of cash inflows and outflows:

Chapter 12

Cash Inflows	Cash Outflows
Product sales to customers	Wages and salaries
Loan proceeds	Purchases
Proceeds from security issues	Taxes
Sale of fixed assets	Debt service
Sale of marketable securities	Dividends
	Purchase of fixed assets
	Purchase of marketable securities

Cash budgeting is the process of forecasting cash inflows and outflows. The cash budget is a time-based (daily, weekly, monthly) schedule of expected cash receipts and disbursements.

■ The following calculations summarize the cash budget:

    Cash inflows
    <u>Less cash outflows</u>
    Net cash gain (loss)
    <u>Add beginning cash balance</u>
    Ending cash balance

■ Knowledge of the expected ending cash balance allows the financial manager time to apply for loans or to liquidate assets in the case of a shortfall, or to invest in marketable securities or to pay down loan balances in the event the company has excess cash.

■ For example, suppose you are the financial manager of FGH Enterprises and are preparing a cash budget for the next three months. Sales in the next three months are expected to be $15,000, $10,000, and $12,000, respectively. Thirty percent of sales revenue is collected in the month of the sale, and the balance is collected during the month following the sale. The company had sales of $10,000 in the month preceding the budgetary period.

Purchases amount to 80 percent of sales for each month, with the payments being made in the following month. Other cash outlays each month are expected to be equal to 5 percent of sales for that month. FGH must repay a loan of $7,000 in the third month. The beginning cash balance is $6,000, which is $500 above the desired minimum cash balance for transactions and precautionary needs.

The cash budget for FGH is as follows:

	Month 1	Month 2	Month 3
Sales	$15,000	$10,000	$12,000
Cash inflows			
Sales (30% current month)	$ 4,500	$ 3,000	$ 3,600
Sales (70% previous month)	7,000	10,500	7,000
Total cash inflows	$11,500	$13,500	$10,600
Cash outflows			
Payments (80% previous month's sales)	$ 8,000	$12,000	$ 8,000
Other outlays (5% current month's sales)	750	500	600
Loan repayment			7,000
Total cash outflows	$8,750	$12,500	$15,600
Net cash gain (loss)	$ 2,750	$ 1,000	($5,000)
Add beginning cash	6,000	8,750	9,750
Ending cash	$ 8,750	$ 9,750	($ 4,750)
Desired balance	$ 5,500	$ 5,500	$ 5,500
Cumulative cash invested (borrowed)	$ 3,250	$ 4,250	($ 750)

FGH anticipates excess cash in both the first and second month. However, the loan repayment due in the third month causes a cash shortage, and arrangements will have to be made to cover it.

By speeding up cash inflows and controlling cash outflows, the financial manager keeps company cash working in more profitable assets such as marketable securities and operating assets. Using *float time* **to the company's advantage is one way financial managers control cash flows.**

- *Collection float time* is the time required for a company to collect cash after a customer issues a check for payment to the company. *Disbursement float time* is the time required for cash to be subtracted from the company's checking account after it issues a check for payment to a supplier. Good cash management involves the minimization of collection float time and the maximization of disbursement float time, subject to legal and ethical considerations.

- Collection and disbursement float time depend largely on mailing time, processing time, and check-clearing time. Check-clearing time has been reduced by recent legislation requiring the Federal Reserve System to clear checks in a maximum of two working days. *Direct sends* reduce check-clearing time even more by bypassing the Federal Reserve System and sending checks directly to correspondent banks for clearing.

Financial managers employ various methods for speeding up cash inflows. To reduce collection float time, companies often use a *lockbox*, which is a post office box rented by a company and serviced by a local bank at which the company keeps an account. Other methods used by companies to speed up cash inflows include:

- Deliver deposits to the bank in person instead of using the mail.

- Deposit receipts on the day they are received.

- Make deposits before the bank's cutoff time for the day.

- Consider factoring accounts receivable.

- Modify terms on credit sales to promote faster payment by customers.

- Mail invoices promptly.

Financial managers employ various methods to control cash outflows. Some methods lengthen disbursement float time while others simply improve the efficiency of handling cash. These include:

- *Remote disbursement*, the practice of drawing a check on a remotely located bank and mailing it from a remote location in order to maximize mailing and clearing times.

Chapter 12

Although legal, this practice raises some ethical considerations.

- Mailing checks at the end of the day.

- Using a *payable through draft (PTD)* instead of a check drawn against a bank.

- Establishing *overdraft* agreements, wherein a bank automatically extends a loan to cover a withdrawal in excess of the company's balance.

- Establishing *zero balance accounts* into which cash is transferred when needed but which otherwise have zero balances.

- Using a *depository transfer check* to move cash from one of the company's banks to another.

Rather than holding cash in a non-interest-bearing account, the financial manager can improve company profitability by investing in money market securities. Criteria considered by financial managers for investing temporarily excess cash include expected rate of return and risk. Risk can be divided into several different categories:

- *Default risk* is the chance that the issuer may default on interest payments or the repayment of principal.

- *Interest rate risk* is the volatility of the investment price due to changes in interest rates.

- *Purchasing-power risk* is the chance that today's dollars will not have as much purchasing-power in the future.

- *Liquidity risk* is the chance that the investment cannot be sold at the prevailing market rate without large transactions costs.

- *Foreign-exchange risk* is the volatility of the price of foreign currency when the cash is invested in foreign securities.

Money market securities generally have low risk in each of these categories. However, safety and liquidity do vary among the various types of money market instruments, and the financial manager must balance these attributes against the promised yields.

Money market securities commonly used for investing temporarily excess cash include:

- *U.S. Treasury bills* -- short-term debt securities issued by the U.S. government.

- *U.S. agency paper* -- short-term debt securities issued by government agencies.

- *Commercial paper* -- short-term promissory notes issued by corporations.

- *Banker's acceptances* -- irrevocable obligations of the accepting bank, which promises to pay the bearer a face amount at maturity.

- *Eurodollar deposits* -- dollar-denominated deposits in banks outside the United States.

- *Foreign short-term securities* -- debt securities issued by foreign companies and countries.

Many financial managers invest excess cash in *repurchase agreements*, **referred to as repos.**

- In a repurchase agreement, a company agrees to purchase a U.S. Treasury bill from a commercial bank with the stipulation that the bank will repurchase it on a specified-date at the then prevailing price. Maturities of repos can be as short as one day or can extend for several months, permitting financial managers to match maturity to company needs.

Companies grant credit to customers to increase sales and profits. When a company sells goods on credit, it creates accounts receivable, a current asset.

- A company must make three principal decisions before granting credit to its customers:

   (1) What credit standards should be used to evaluate customers?

Chapter 12

(2) What credit terms should the company use?

(3) How should the company collect overdue accounts receivable?

Credit standards are the criteria a company uses to determine whether or not a potential customer is creditworthy and whether present customers should continue to receive credit.

■ There is a trade-off between expected benefits and costs associated with extending credit. Expected benefits are the increased profits from incremental sales caused by extending credit. Costs are the increase in expenses necessary to collect slow-paying accounts, bad-debt expense, and the opportunity cost of tying up cash in accounts receivable.

■ Financial managers often use the *five Cs of credit* to determine whether or not an applicant meets the company's credit standards:

Character is the moral fiber of the borrower and gives some indication of the borrower's willingness to honor financial obligations. Credit history provides some insight into an applicant's character.

Capacity refers to the credit applicant's ability to pay. It is generally evaluated on the basis of projected cash flows.

Capital refers to the relative amount of debt and equity of the applicant. A large amount of debt relative to equity is a sign that the applicant is exposed to substantial financial risk.

Collateral is the customer's assets pledged as a promise of repayment. Collateral is seldom used in *trade credit*, the extending of credit by one company to another in the normal course of business.

Conditions refer to special circumstances of the credit-granting company as well as the general economic climate.

■ In an attempt to quantify the five Cs, some financial managers use a system of *credit scoring*. Credit scoring uses discriminant analysis to develop equations that distinguish high-quality applicants from low-quality applicants. Credit scoring is useful in sorting credit applications.

Credit terms, **or terms of sale, tell the customer when to pay for the goods purchased on credit. Some companies offer cash discounts for early payment. The offer creates an opportunity cost for the customer.**

- For example, your company offers credit terms of 3/15, net 45. The terms indicate that customers can take a 3 percent discount on their payments if they pay on or before the 15th day; otherwise, the full amount is due in 45 days. Suppose one particular customer owes $5,000 from purchases last month. The customer can pay $4,850 by the 15th day or pay the full $5,000 in 45 days.

If the customer rejects the discount, he or she is in effect paying $150 for the use of $4,850 for 30 days. The opportunity cost for the 30 days is calculated as:

Opportunity cost for 30 days = $150/$4,850
= 0.0309, or 3.09%

Most financial managers prefer to think of interest rates as annual rates. To change the 30-day rate to an annual rate, multiply it by the number of 30-day periods in a year:

Number of 30-day periods in a year = 365/30
= 12.167

Annual opportunity cost = 0.0309 × 12.167
= 0.376, or 37.6%

The cost of not taking the cash discount is approximately 37.6 percent. Even if the customer did not have the cash to make payment within 15 days, he or she would be better off borrowing the cash to take advantage of the discount *as long as the interest rate on the loan was less than 37.6 percent.*

A one-step equation for calculating the annual opportunity cost of not taking a cash discount is as follows:

$$\text{Annual opportunity cost} = [D/(1 - D)] \times (365/n)$$

where D equals the cash discount percentage *expressed as a decimal*, and n equals the number of days during the period between the deadline for cash discount and final payment.

- For the above example, the one-step formula would be:

$$\text{Annual opportunity cost} = [0.03/(1 - 0.03)] \times (365/30)$$
$$= .0309 \times 12.167$$
$$= 0.376, \text{ or } 37.6\%$$

To minimize the investment in accounts receivable, the financial manager must compare the opportunity cost of not taking the cash discount to customers' borrowing costs.

- If the opportunity cost of not taking the cash discount exceeds customer borrowing rates, customers should pay early to take advantage of the discount, even if it means borrowing from the bank to do so. This will help to minimize the company's investment in accounts receivable. Financial managers may have to adjust credit terms periodically to keep the opportunity cost of not taking the discount higher than the general level of interest rates to encourage prompt payment.

The effect of a company's credit terms on its accounts receivable can be monitored using two basic ratios:

$$\text{Accounts receivable turnover} = \text{Credit sales/Accounts receivable}$$

- The accounts receivable turnover measures the dollar amount of credit sales per dollar of receivables. If customers stop taking cash discounts because of relatively higher borrowing costs, the accounts receivable of the credit-granting company will increase, causing its receivables turnover to decrease.

$$\text{Average collection period} = \text{Accounts receivable/Average daily credit sales}$$

- The average collection period represents the average number of days required to collect credit sales. It can also be calculated by dividing 365 days by the accounts receivable turnover.

- For example, suppose your company generates annual credit sales of $625,000 and has an average accounts receivable balance of $76,027. Accounts receivable turnover would be:

$$\text{Accounts receivable turnover} = \$625,000/\$76,027$$
$$= 8.22 \text{ times per year}$$

Average collection period (ACP) would be:

$$\text{ACP} = \$76,027/(\$625,000/365)$$
$$= \$76,027/\$1,712$$
$$= 44.4 \text{ days}$$

Alternatively, the average collection period could be calculated as:

$$\text{ACP} = 365/8.22$$
$$= 44.4 \text{ days}$$

- The financial manager can use either or both of these ratios to asses the way credit terms alter the company's accounts receivable. Low receivables turnover and long average collection period indicate a buildup of receivables, suggesting that credit policy needs to be reviewed.

A company's *collection practices*, the methods it uses to collect receivables, are an important part of the company's credit policy.

- Most companies base collection procedures on a series of periodic and gradually stronger reminders to customers that payment is due. A *dunning notice* is a letter to a credit customer urging immediate payment.

- Delay and inattention in the collection process can be costly and ultimately lead to increased *bad-debt expense*. Bad debts reflect sales made but not collected, causing the seller to lose the cost of the goods and the expected profit.

- The collection pattern of receivables can be assessed by classifying accounts according to the length of time they have been outstanding. This is referred to as *aging receivables*. The value of a receivable declines as it ages because the probability of collection declines and also because of the time value of money.

- Possible action on overdue accounts includes (1) continue the collection effort, (2) turn over the account to a collection agency, or (3) write off the account as bad-debt expense.

Inventory is a current asset that companies use to support sales and production. The functions of inventory management are :

- To maintain levels of inventory adequate to meet demand.

- To order or produce more inventory when stocks run low.

- To order or produce sufficient quantities to avoid shortages.

The role of inventory is clarified by considering the three types of inventory.

- *Raw materials inventory* is the basic input to a company's production process. Holding raw materials inventory creates an independence between the purchasing and production departments and prevents delays in production. Raw materials are usually financially liquid because a company can sell them quickly to other companies to use in their production.

- *Work-in-process inventory* consists of partially finished products being produced by a company. Longer assembly lines require more work-in-process inventory than do shorter ones to maintain a constant flow of output. Work in process is the least liquid part of inventory because it cannot easily be sold to other companies for use in their production.

- *Finished goods inventory* consists of products that are available for sale. Holding finished goods inventory reduces the dependency of sales on production. With finished goods inventory, the company can also meet unexpected demand.

Inventory costs fall into four categories: (1) cost of designing and implementing the inventory control system, (2) stockout costs, (3) cost of ordering inventory, and (4) cost of carrying inventory.

Chapter 12

- The *cost of designing and implementing an inventory control system* includes the cost of (1) system design and acquisition of computer capacity to keep track of products stored in inventory, and (2) incremental salaries to staff the system.

- *Stockout costs*, or shortage costs, occur when a company loses sales because of insufficient inventory of finished goods, or when a company must shut down a production line because of insufficient raw materials and work-in-process inventories.

- *Ordering costs*, or setup costs, are the administrative expenses associated with an order. These costs are largely independent of the size of the order.

- *Carrying costs* are the outlays required to hold inventory. They rise as the dollar size of the inventory increases. Examples of carrying costs include cost of capital tied up in inventory, storage costs, obsolescence, taxes, and insurance.

Ordering costs over a period vary inversely with carrying costs.

Since the costs of carrying and ordering inventory are unavoidable for most companies, the task of the financial manager is to determine a level of inventory that will minimize the total of the two costs.

- Carrying costs can be calculated as:

$$\text{Carrying costs} = A \times C$$

where A equals average size of inventory in units and C equals the annual cost to carry one unit of inventory.

- Ordering costs can be calculated as:

$$\text{Ordering costs} = N \times O$$

where N equals number of orders placed per year and O equals the cost to place one order.

- Putting these costs together yields the following equation for total costs:

Chapter 12

$$\text{Total costs} = (A \times C) + (N \times O)$$

- The trade-off between ordering costs and carrying costs becomes apparent: (1) placing a small number of large orders causes ordering costs to be small and carrying costs to be large; (2) placing a large number of small orders causes ordering costs to be large and carrying costs to be small.

The *economic order quantity (EOQ)* is the quantity of inventory units ordered that minimizes the sum of carrying costs and ordering costs.

$$EOQ = \sqrt{(2 \times S \times O)/C}$$

where S equals sales per year in units of inventory.

- For example, Gene's Greenhouse sells 3,600 geraniums per year and wants to know the economic order quantity. Each geranium costs Gene's $6, and cash ordering costs are $12 per order. Annual carrying costs are estimated at 25 percent of the purchase price, or $1.50 per geranium. EOQ is calculated as follows:

$$EOQ = \sqrt{(2 \times 3{,}600 \times \$12)/\$1.50}$$
$$= 240 \text{ geraniums}$$

- If Gene's uses the EOQ model, the number of orders placed per year (N) would be equal to sales (S) divided by EOQ:

$$N = S/EOQ$$
$$= 3{,}600/240$$
$$= 15 \text{ orders}$$

- If a company uses the EOQ model and sells inventory evenly over time, the average inventory in units is the EOQ divided by 2:

$$\text{Average inventory (A)} = EOQ/2$$

For Gene's Greenhouse, the average inventory would be:

Chapter 12

$$A = 240/2$$
$$= 120 \text{ geraniums}$$

- Total carrying costs equal the carrying cost per unit times the average number of inventory units. For Gene's, this would be:

$$\text{Total carrying costs} = \$1.50 \times 120$$
$$= \$180$$

- Total ordering costs are the cost per order times the number of orders placed during the year. For Gene's, this would be:

$$\text{Total ordering costs} = \$12 \times 15$$
$$= \$180$$

- Total inventory costs, based on the EOQ, are the sum of total carrying costs and total ordering costs. For Gene's, this would be:

$$\text{Total costs} = \$180 + \$180$$
$$= \$360$$

To prove that EOQ yields the minimum total costs, change the number of units the company orders and recalculate the total costs. Any other quantity ordered will result in total costs greater than $360.

To avoid stockouts, an inventory control system relies on the *order point* and *safety stock*.

- The *order point* is the level of remaining inventory at which management places an order (EOQ) for additional units. The order point depends on how rapidly the company uses inventory and the delivery time.

$$\text{Order Point (OP)} = S \times L$$

where S equals sales per day and L equals the lead time required for delivery.

- For example, if Gene's Greenhouse is open 300 days per year, and it takes 4 days to

Chapter 12

obtain a delivery of geraniums, the order point for additional geraniums would be:

$$OP = (3{,}600/300) \times 4 \text{ days}$$
$$= 48 \text{ geraniums}$$

- *Safety stock* is a cushion against the uncertainty surrounding sales levels and delivery times. Companies hold safety stock to prevent stockouts. Holding safety stock increases the average size of inventory and inventory carrying costs, but it does not affect the EOQ.

- If Gene's Greenhouse determines that a safety stock of 12 geraniums is needed, the order point would be:

$$OP = (S \times L) + \text{Safety stock}$$
$$= 48 + 12$$
$$= 60 \text{ geraniums}$$

For Gene's, the addition of a safety stock of 12 geraniums increases average inventory from 120 to 132. Average inventory carrying costs would increase from $180 to $198.

Financial managers use other methods in addition to the EOQ model to manage inventory.

- In the *ABC system*, inventory is classified into one of three groups: A, B, or C. The A group would contain the inventory items requiring the closest scrutiny: high-cost and high-volume items. Groups B and C would contain second- and third-priority items.

- The *80-20 rule* suggests that 80 percent of a company's sales come from 20 percent of the inventory. These items would be in group A, garnering the most attention from the financial manager.

A company's success in controlling its inventory is reflected in its *inventory turnover*.

- Inventory turnover is the amount of sales (measured at cost) per dollar of inventory:

$$\text{Inventory turnover} = \text{Cost of goods sold}/\text{Inventory}$$

Given the information above for Gene's Greenhouse, the inventory turnover for geraniums is calculated as:

$$\text{Cost of goods sold} = 3{,}600 \times \$6$$
$$= \$21{,}600$$

$$\text{Inventory value} = 132 \times \$6$$
$$= \$792$$

$$\text{Inventory turnover} = \$21{,}600/\$792$$
$$= 27.3 \text{ times per year}$$

Whether 27.3 times per year is a good ratio for Gene's depends on the industry average. A ratio substantially different from the industry average is a red flag telling the financial manager that the company should evaluate its inventory control.

A recent innovation in inventory management, the just-in-time (JIT) system, was developed in Japan.

A JIT system attempts to reduce the investment in inventory by coordinating purchasing and manufacturing activities so that raw materials arrive at a work station just in time for processing. JIT systems push inventories back to suppliers instead of holding them in the company.

Current liabilities, or short-term debts, provide temporary funds to companies when cash inflows from operations do not match cash needs. The largest source of short-term financing for most companies is accounts payable, also referred to as *trade credit*. Trade credit is credit extended by one company to another in the normal course of business. A company receives trade credit when it buys goods from a supplier without paying cash on or before delivery.

- Companies establish *open-book relationships* with their customers after completing credit checks, arranging credit lines, and setting credit terms. If a company is uncertain about the creditworthiness of a customer, the customer may be required to sign a *promissory note*, which is a legal document for an IOU.

- Competition among sellers and industry standards and customs largely control the

Chapter 12

credit terms a customer receives. Companies also take into account the payment record and financial position of their customers, granting customers with good payment records and sound financial positions more trade credit than their weaker counterparts.

The dollar size of accounts payable depends on the size of daily purchases and the number of days before the purchaser makes payment. The number of days before payment depends on the credit terms and the purchaser's payment behavior. When a company extends its payment period beyond the due date of the credit terms, it is *stretching accounts payable.*

- By stretching accounts payable, a customer lessens the need for bank loans and reduces interest expense.

- There are costs associated with stretching accounts payable, however. Slow payment behavior increases the risk of ruining a company's credit rating, resulting in more restrictive credit terms. Additionally, a company may lose cash discounts offered for prompt payment.

Commercial banks provide the second largest total dollar volume of short-term funds in the form of secured and unsecured loans. Secured loans guarantee interest and principal repayment with pledged assets. Unsecured loans do not require the pledging of assets to secure them. Examples of unsecured loans include:

- A *direct loan* is a one-time loan negotiated with a bank for a specific purpose. Direct loans are commonly used to finance seasonal bulges in current assets.

- To assure that loans from banks will be available when needed, companies often establish a *line of credit* with one or more banks. A line of credit is an informal agreement establishing the maximum amount a company may borrow during a year. The company can draw (borrow) against the line throughout the year without delay.

Banks generally require the borrower to reapply for a line of credit each year. In addition, the credit line may have an *annual cleanup* provision which prohibits the borrower from using the line for some specified period (usually 30 consecutive days) during the year.

- A *revolving credit agreement* is a formal agreement between a company and a bank that establishes the maximum loan balance permissible during a period of time. The revolving credit agreement differs from a line of credit in that:

1. A revolving agreement is a legal commitment that cannot be canceled by the bank; banks may cancel lines of credit at any time.
2. Banks charge a commitment fee to maintain a revolving credit agreement; there is no fee for the line of credit.
3. A revolving credit agreement may extend beyond one year; a line of credit is subject to annual renewal.
4. The annual cleanup restriction of the line of credit does not apply to a revolving credit agreement.

In addition to charging borrowers interest on short-term loans, many banks require the borrower to maintain a *compensating balance* as a condition for the loan.

- A compensating balance is a cash deposit kept at the bank, required primarily for unsecured loans. The size of the compensating balance is usually stated as a percentage of the amount borrowed or of the size of the loan commitment.

The *true cost* of a bank loan depends on the amount of cash received by the borrower and the timing and amount of cash paid by the borrower.

- The true cost of a bank loan is rarely the stated, or *nominal*, interest rate that the bank quotes. In most cases, the true, or *effective*, rate exceeds the nominal rate because of compensating balance requirements and the timing of interest payments.

On *simple interest* loans for one year with no compensating balance requirement, the effective annual rate of interest is equal to the nominal rate.

- For example, suppose that Imelda's Shoe Shop borrows $150,000 from The Change Bank ("we make change") for a 1-year period. A compensating balance is not required, and the loan carries a 14 percent annual interest rate. The effective annual rate of the loan is:

$$\begin{aligned} \text{Interest} &= \text{Principal} \times \text{Rate} \times \text{Time} \\ &= \$150{,}000 \times 0.14 \times 1 \text{ year} \\ &= \$21{,}000 \end{aligned}$$

Usable proceeds = $150,000

Effective annual rate = Interest/Usable loan proceeds
= $21,000/$150,000
= 0.14, or 14% per year compounded annually

A *discount-interest loan* requires that interest be paid in advance rather than at the end of the loan period. The bank deducts interest from the loan principal, and the borrower repays the principal at maturity. With discount interest, the usable loan proceeds are less than the loan principal by the amount of the interest.

■ For Imelda's Shoe Shop, if The Change Bank charges 14 percent discount interest on a $150,000 loan for one year, the effective annual rate is calculated as:

Discount interest = $150,000 × 0.14 × 1 year
= $21,000

Usable loan proceeds = $150,000 - $21,000 = $129,000

Effective annual rate = $21,000/$129,000
= 0.163, or 16.3% per year compounded annually

For a simple-interest loan with a compensating balance requirement, the company pays interest on the total borrowed, but it cannot use the total borrowed because of the compensating balance requirement. This raises the effective annual rate.

■ For Imelda's Shoe Shop, the effective annual rate for a 1-year, 14 percent simple-interest $150,000 loan with a 10 percent compensating balance requirement would be calculated as follows:

Interest = $150,000 × 0.14 × 1 year
= $21,000

Compensating balance = $150,000 × 0.10
= $15,000

Usable loan proceeds = $150,000 - $15,000
= $135,000

Effective annual rate = $21,000/$135,000
= 0.156, or 15.6% per year compounded annually

If a company is required to keep a compensating balance *and* pay discount-interest, the effective annual rate increases even more.

- For Imelda's Shoe Shop, paying discount-interest on a 1-year loan for $150,000 at 14 percent nominal interest with a 10 percent compensating balance requirement would result in the following effective annual rate:

Interest = $150,000 × 0.14 × 1 year
= $21,000

Compensating balance = $150,000 × 0.10
= $15,000

Usable loan proceeds = $150,000 - ($21,000 + $15,000)
= $114,000

Effective annual rate = $21,000/$114,000
= 0.184, or 18.4% per year compounded annually

Many short-term loans are secured with collateral consisting of accounts receivable or inventory.

- Companies turn to secured loans for several reasons: (1) A company may be too new to have established a strong credit history that will qualify it for an unsecured loan; (2) a company's credit history may be weak; or (3) a company may have used up its unsecured borrowing capacity.

Some companies pledge accounts receivable as collateral for secured loans from commercial banks or finance companies.

- The amount of the loan depends on the lender's assessment of the quality of the receivables. Lenders typically limit loans to between 50 and 80 percent of the book value of the pledged receivables. If the borrower's customers default, the lender has legal recourse against the borrower.

Instead of pledging accounts receivable under a loan arrangement, some companies choose to *factor receivables*.

- Factoring is the outright sale of receivables. The companies that buy the receivables are called *factors*. Examples of factors include bank holding companies, finance companies, and companies that specialize in factoring. Factoring is very common in the finished apparel, textile products, and furniture manufacturing industries.

- A factor performs three functions: (1) credit checking of the seller's customers, (2) risk bearing -- the factor assumes responsibility for collection and bad-debts, and (3) lending cash to the seller prior to collection of the receivables. Factors charge a fee for credit checking and risk bearing, normally one to three percent of the receivables. For the lending function, they typically charge prime plus two to four percentage points.

Loans secured by a company's inventory are called *inventory loans*. Inventory loan arrangements include floating liens, trust receipts, and warehouse receipts. The procedure lenders select depends on the physical characteristics of the inventory.

- A *floating lien* grants the lender a lien against all of the borrower's inventory. The inventory remains in the borrower's possession, who conducts business as usual. The lender has no control over the inventory and must wait until the termination of the loan to receive payment. Because of the default risk involved, the lender will carefully check the borrower's creditworthiness before agreeing to the arrangement.

- Under a *trust receipt loan*, borrower give the lender signed trust receipts acknowledging that designated inventory is held in trust for the lender. Trust receipts are used only for items that the lender can easily identify. Receipts from the sale of the designated items are used to repay the loan. Trust receipts give the lender more control than does a floating lien. Still, it is in the lender's best interest to periodically inspect the inventory.

- Under a *warehouse receipt* arrangement, the lender has a lien against specific inventory stored in a warehouse. With *public warehousing*, the inventory is placed in a public warehouse and is released only on the lender's authorization. In *field warehousing*, the lender stores pledged inventory on the borrowing company's premises and employs a custodian to control the flow of inventory in and out of the controlled area. Warehouse receipt financing has the added cost of inventory handling and storage.

GLOSSARY OF KEY TERMS

80-20 rule: rule of thumb that a company makes 80 percent of sales from 20 percent of inventory items

ABC system: system for monitoring inventory levels based on prioritized groups of items

accounts receivable turnover: dollar amount of credit sales per dollar of receivables

aging receivables: classifying accounts based on length of time they have been uncollected

annual cleanup: loan provision requiring the borrower to be out of debt to the bank for at least 30 consecutive days during a 12-month period

average collection period: average time required to collect receivables; days' sales in accounts receivable

carrying costs: costs of holding inventory; includes cost of capital, storage costs, obsolescence, taxes, and insurance

cash budget: schedule of expected cash inflows and outflows

cash budgeting: process of forecasting cash inflows and outflows

collection float: dollar amount of cash inflows in transit to a company

collection float time: time required to collect cash after a customer issues a check

commitment fee: dollar amount charged by a bank to maintain a revolving credit agreement

Chapter 12

compensating balance: cash in a bank account as a condition for obtaining a bank loan or service

credit scoring: quantifying an applicant's creditworthiness

credit standards: criteria for determining a customer's creditworthiness

credit terms: terms of sale; conditions to which a customer must agree in order to receive credit

depository transfer check (DTC): check used to transfer cash from a company's account at one bank to its account at another bank

direct loan: negotiated bank loan intended for a specific purpose; one-time loan

direct send: mechanism to reduce check-clearing time; bypasses the Federal Reserve and sends checks directly to a correspondent bank for clearing

disbursement float: dollar amount of cash outflows in transit from a company

disbursement float time: time required for a payer's bank to reduce the checking balance after the payer issues a check

discount-interest loan: borrower pays interest in advance; contrasts with a simple-interest loan in which the borrower pays interest at maturity

dunning notice: letter to a credit customer urging immediate payment

economic order quantity (EOQ): quantity of inventory units ordered that minimizes the sum of carrying costs and ordering costs

factor receivables: sell receivables to a financial institution for cash

field warehousing: pledged inventory maintained on the borrower's premises

finished goods inventory: products ready to sell; stock in trade available for sale

floating lien: legal claim against all of a company's inventory

inventory turnover: dollar amount of sales (at cost) per dollar of inventory; cost of goods sold divided by inventory

inventory loan: loan secured by a company's inventory

just-in-time (JIT) system: system that tries to move inventory to the production line as close as possible to the time it is needed

line of credit: informal agreement establishing the maximum amount a company may borrow during a year

lockbox: post office box rented by a company and serviced by a local bank

order point: quantity of remaining inventory units at which management orders the EOQ

ordering costs: costs of ordering inventory; includes cost of preparing purchase orders and follow-up work, receiving, and processing orders

overdraft: withdrawal of money in excess of the company's deposit balance

payable through draft (PTD): written order to pay cash to the payee only after the payer agrees to the order

planning balance: cash held for expected capital expenditures
precautionary balance: cash held to protect against emergencies
promissory note: legal document for an IOU
public warehousing: pledged inventory maintained in an off-premise warehouse
raw materials inventory: basic inputs of materials to a company's production process
remote disbursement: drawing a check on a remotely located bank and mailing it from a remote location to maximize disbursement float time
revolving credit agreement: formal agreement establishing the maximum amount a company may borrow during a period of time
safety stock (SS): precautionary balance of inventory to prevent stockouts
speculative balance: cash held to take advantage of unexpected opportunities
stockout costs: lost profit on lost sales attributable to inadequate inventory
stretching accounts payable: delaying payment beyond the due date of the credit terms
trade credit: credit extended by one company to another in the normal course of business
transactions balance: cash held to meet payments because of timing differences between cash inflows and outflows
trust receipt: legal claim against specific inventory items with identification numbers
usable loan proceeds: cash available from a loan for the borrower's use
warehouse receipt: legal claim against specific inventory in a warehouse
work-in-process inventory: partially finished products being produced by a company
zero balance accounts: bank accounts into which cash is transferred when needed but which otherwise have zero balances

Chapter 12

MULTIPLE CHOICE SELF-TEST

1. A company's cash balance may consist of all of the following except

    a. a planning balance
    b. a speculative balance
    c. a compensating balance
    d. an inflationary balance
    e. a precautionary balance

2. A company's cash balance increases immediately when it

    a. sells a product on credit
    b. purchases a U.S. Treasury bill
    c. collects a receivable
    d. retires a bond
    e. buys office supplies

3. The cash budget is a

    a. historical statement of cash flows
    b. short-term planning tool
    c. subdivision of the capital budget
    d. part of a standard set of audited financial statements
    e. summary of future cash flows known with certainty

4. In general, a financial manager would like to _____ cash inflows and _____ cash outflows.

    a. reduce; increase
    b. speed up; delay
    c. slow down; eliminate
    d. accelerate; accelerate
    e. concentrate; disperse

220

Chapter 12

5. The purpose of a lockbox is to

   a. reduce collection float time
   b. increase collection float time
   c. reduce disbursement float time
   d. increase disbursement float time
   e. increase sales

6. Which of the following would be used to increase disbursement float time?

   a. factor accounts receivable
   b. mail checks at the end of the day
   c. use a lockbox
   d. mail invoices promptly
   e. deposit receipts on the day they are received

7. When investing temporarily excess cash, financial managers

   a. attempt to obtain the highest possible expected return
   b. attempt to eliminate all risks
   c. consider both risk and return
   d. primarily invest in low-risk stocks and bonds
   e. have no constraints

8. The five Cs of credit include all of the following except

   a. character
   b. compensation
   c. conditions
   d. capacity
   e. capital

221

Chapter 12

9. The quantification of the likelihood that a credit applicant will pay is called

   a. credit terms
   b. credit selection
   c. credit policy
   d. credit scoring
   e. credit standards

10. Credit terms are typically expressed in a form similar to

    a. 30, net 2/10
    b. 5/10/15
    c. 5/10, net 25
    d. 10 net, less 2
    e. 2/10, COD

11. Ideally, accounts receivable turnover is the ratio of _____ to accounts receivable.

    a. total sales
    b. credit sales
    c. cost of goods sold
    d. purchases
    e. inventory

12. The economic order quantity model minimizes the sum of

    a. ordering costs and carrying costs
    b. variable costs and fixed costs
    c. selling costs and purchasing costs
    d. sunk costs and marginal costs
    e. production costs and marketing costs

Chapter 12

13. Placing a smaller number of larger orders would generally

    a. eliminate ordering costs and accelerate carrying costs
    b. increase ordering costs and decrease carrying costs
    c. delay ordering costs and prevent carrying costs
    d. override ordering costs and implement carrying costs
    e. decrease ordering costs and increase carrying costs

14. Which of the following is not a form of short-term financing?

    a. line of credit
    b. factoring
    c. trade credit
    d. bond financing
    e. floating lien

15. Which of the following forms of short-term financing does not involve negotiation with a bank?

    a. direct loan
    b. line of credit
    c. trade credit
    d. revolving credit agreement
    e. none of the above

16. When a company factors its receivables,

    a. it retains title to them
    b. it continues to do credit analysis of its customers
    c. its bad-debt expenses go up
    d. its average collection period goes to zero
    e. it can borrow 100 percent of the receivables from the factor

223

Chapter 12

PROBLEMS

Use the following information for Problems 1 to 6:

You are the controller for a mail-order distributor of computer and office supplies. Your task is to prepare a 4-month cash budget for the company. You have the following information:

Sales for the next four months are expected to be $38,000, $44,000, $45,000 and $45,000, respectively. Sales were $34,000 last month and $30,000 two months ago. Twenty percent of sales are paid for in cash. The remainder is carried on account. Twenty percent of credit sales are collected in the month of the sale, 50 percent in the first month following the sale, and the remainder in the second month following the sale.

Purchases for a given month average 80 percent of sales. Twenty percent of purchases are paid in the month of the purchase, and the remainder is paid in the first month following the sale. Miscellaneous monthly outlays are expected to be $9,000.

On the last day of the month preceding the forecast period, the cash balance was $8,000. You wish to have a cash balance of $8,000 at the end of each month. Any shortage will be covered by the sale of marketable securities, or by short-term bank loans if marketable securities have been depleted. Any excess will be used to repay any short-term borrowing, or will be invested in marketable securities if no short-term loans are outstanding. At the beginning of the forecast period, the company had no short-term borrowing and had $5,000 invested in marketable securities. Ignore interest payments on short-term loans and interest received on marketable securities.

1. What will be the cash inflow during the first month of the cash budget from the collection of accounts receivable?

2. What will be the total cash inflow during the third month of the cash budget?

3. What will be the cash outflow for purchases during the first month of the cash budget?

4. What will be the total cash outflow during the fourth month of the cash budget?

5. What will be the cumulative short-term borrowing or investment position of the company at the end of the first month?

6. What will be the cumulative short-term borrowing or investment position of the company at the end of the fourth month?

7. Your company offers its customers credit terms of 1/10, net 45. Current borrowing costs for your customers average 15 percent annual interest. If you would like to improve your company's cash flow, which of the following changes in credit terms would be the better choice: (1) 1/10, net 60, or (2) 1/10, net 30?

8. Egbert Emery is a wholesaler of surfing and sailing supplies. His company, Emery Boards, sells 4,000 units of water shoes per year. Ordering costs are $20 per order, and carrying costs are $1 per unit. Calculate the EOQ for Emery Boards.

9. Fonzorelli Foods needs to borrow a net amount of $1,000,000 and is considering 4 alternatives offered by The Second City National Bank:

   Alternative A: 1-year loan, simple interest, 15 percent nominal rate.
   Alternative B: 1-year loan, discount interest, 12.5 percent nominal rate.
   Alternative C: 1-year loan, simple interest, 11.6 percent nominal rate, 20 percent compensating balance requirement.
   Alternative D: 1-year loan, discount interest, 12.6 percent nominal rate, 10 percent compensating balance requirement.

   Calculate the effective annual cost of each alternative. Which one should Fonzorelli Foods choose?

Chapter 12

SOLUTIONS TO MULTIPLE CHOICE SELF-TEST

1. d	5. a	9. d	13. e
2. c	6. b	10. c	14. d
3. b	7. c	11. b	15. c
4. b	8. b	12. a	16. d

SOLUTIONS TO PROBLEMS

The following cash budget is used to answer Problems 1 to 6:

Month	1	2	3	4
Sales	$38,000	$44,000	$45,000	$45,000
Cash sales	7,600	8,800	9,000	9,000
20% of A/R	6,080	7,040	7,200	7,200
50% of A/R	13,600	15,200	17,600	18,000
30% of A/R	7,200	8,160	9,120	10,560
Total inflow	$34,480	$39,200	$42,920	$44,760
Purchases	$30,400	$35,200	$36,000	$36,000
20% of A/P	6,080	7,040	7,200	7,200
80% of A/P	21,760	24,320	28,160	28,800
Misc.	9,000	9,000	9,000	9,000
Total outflow	$36,840	$40,360	$44,360	$45,000
Net cash gain (loss)	($2,360)	($1,160)	($1,440)	($240)
Add beginning cash balance	8,000	5,640	4,480	3,040
Ending cash balance	5,640	4,480	3,040	2,800
Less cash balance desired	8,000	8,000	8,000	8,000
Cumulative cash invested (borrowed)	($2,360)	($3,520)	($4,960)	($5,200)

Chapter 12

1. Collection of A/R in Month 1:
   $6,080 + $13,600 + $7,200 = $26,880

2. Total cash inflow in Month 3:
   $42,920 (see above)

3. Cash outflow from A/P in Month 1:
   $6,080 + $21,760 = $27,840

4. Total cash outflow in Month 4:
   $45,000 (see above)

5. In Month 1, $2,360 of the $5,000 in marketable securities will have to be sold off, leaving $2,640 invested.

6. In Month 4, the remaining $40 of marketable securities will have to be sold off, and an additional $200 borrowed.

7. Annual opportunity cost of 1/10, net 45 = $0.01/0.99 \times 365/35$
   $= 0.105$, or 10.5%

   Annual opportunity cost of 1/10, net 60 = $0.01/0.99 \times 365/50$
   $= 0.074$, or 7.4%

   Annual opportunity cost of 1/10, net 30 = $0.01/0.99 \times 365/20$
   $= 0.184$, or 18.4%

   If the company wants customers to take the cash discount, it will have to make the cost of forgoing the discount greater than the customers' borrowing costs. Therefore, the terms 1/10, net 30 should be adopted since the opportunity cost of 18.4% exceeds customers' borrowing costs of 15%.

8. $EOQ = \sqrt{(2 \times S \times O)/C}$

Chapter 12

$$= \sqrt{(2 \times 4{,}000 \times \$20)/\$1}$$

$$= 400 \text{ units}$$

9. Alternative A:
   Interest = $1,000,000 × 0.15
           = $150,000
   Usable loan proceeds = $1,000,000
   Effective annual rate = $150,000/$1,000,000 = 0.15

   Alternative B:
   Interest = $1,000,000 × 0.125
           = $125,000
   Usable loan proceeds = $1,000,000 - $125,000
                         = $875,000
   Effective annual rate = $125,000/$875,000 = 0.143

   Alternative C:
   Interest = $1,000,000 × 0.116
           = $116,000
   Compensating balance = $1,000,000 × 0.20
                          = $200,000
   Usable loan proceeds = $1,000,000 - $200,000
                         = $800,000
   Effective annual rate = $116,000/$800,000 = 0.145

   Alternative D:
   Interest = $1,000,000 × 0.126
           = $126,000
   Compensating balance = $1,000,000 × 0.10
                          = $100,000
   Usable loan proceeds = $1,000,000 - ($126,000 + $100,000)
                         = $774,000
   Effective annual rate = $126,000/$774,000 = 0.163

   Alternative B has the lowest effective annual rate.

13 ANALYZING FINANCIAL PERFORMANCE

OVERVIEW

Financial managers have an obvious interest in analyzing a company's financial condition and performance. A company's suppliers, creditors, and shareholders share this interest because they need assurances that their stakes in the company are secure. This chapter describes how stakeholders assess the financial strengths and weaknesses of a company through analysis of its financial statements. The company's income statement and balance sheet are used to develop financial ratios that relate information about company profitability, asset management, debt management, and liquidity. Trends in the ratios and comparisons of them with industry averages reveal the financial strengths and weaknesses within the company.

OUTLINE

Financial managers, suppliers, creditors, and shareholders use financial ratios to analyze a company's financial condition and performance. Interpreting these ratios requires a standard for comparison. The most commonly used standards in financial-statement analysis are developed from trend analysis and industry averages.

- *Trend analysis* compares a financial ratio with itself at an earlier point in time. Consistent application of accounting principles produces financial statements that are comparable over time, so financial ratios calculated from these statements are also comparable. Upward or downward trends provide the analyst with the general pattern

Chapter 13

of a company's performance.

- *Industry comparative analysis* is the process of comparing a company's ratios with industry average ratios. Analysts must use care in selecting the industry used for comparison. Product lines and total asset size should be similar in order to obtain meaningful comparisons.

- Used in combination with trend analysis, industry comparative analysis enables the analyst to identify managerial (internal) versus environmental (external) influences on company performance.

- Industry average figures are available in several publications, including the following:

    Annual Statement Studies, published by Robert Morris Associates (RMA), an association of bank loan officers.

    Key Business Ratios, published by Dun & Bradstreet.

    Quarterly Financial Report for Manufacturing Companies, published by the Federal Trade Commission and the Securities and Exchange Commission.

    Almanac of Business and Industrial Financial Ratios, published by Prentice-Hall.

    Industry Surveys, published by Standard & Poor's.

    In the absence of published industry averages, the analyst may need to compile averages from similar companies before undertaking the analysis.

Assessing the financial strengths and weaknesses of a company requires four groups of financial ratios: profitability ratios, asset management ratios, debt management ratios, and liquidity ratios.

- These ratios are developed from information contained in a company's income statement and balance sheet. To illustrate the calculation and interpretation of these ratios, we will use the financial statements for Mal-Mart Corporation:

Chapter 13

Balance Sheet for Year Ending December 31, 1997

Assets

Cash	$ 96,600
Marketable securities	50,000
Accounts receivable	83,400
Inventory	110,000
Total current assets	$340,000
Fixed assets (net of depreciation)	305,000
Total assets	$645,000

Liabilities and Shareholder Equity

Accounts payable	$ 56,000
Notes payable	30,000
Current portion of long-term debt	20,000
Total current liabilities	$106,000
Long-term debt	184,000
Total liabilities	$290,000
Common stock (50,000 shares)	180,000
Paid-in capital in excess of par	100,000
Retained earnings	75,000
Total shareholder equity	$355,000
Total liabilities and equity	$645,000

Income Statement for Year Ending December 31, 1997

Net sales (93% on credit)	$760,000
Cost of goods sold	437,000
Gross profit	$323,000
Operating expenses	152,000
Earnings before interest and taxes	$171,000
Interest expense	37,000
Earnings before taxes	$134,000
Income taxes	39,500
Earnings after taxes	$ 94,500

Chapter 13

Profitability ratios measure the effectiveness of all managerial policies and decisions.

■ A *profit margin* is developed using data from the income statement only and represents profit per dollar of sales.

■ A *return on investment* is developed using data from both the income statement and the balance sheet and represents profit per dollar of investment.

■ A *common-size income statement* is an income statement with all items expressed as a percentage of sales. Common-size income statements over several years are useful for analyzing trends in both profit margins and expense percentages.

Commonly used profit margins include (1) gross profit margin, (2) EBIT margin, (3) before-tax profit margin, and (4) after-tax profit margin.

■ The *gross profit margin* shows gross profit per dollar of net sales:

$$\begin{aligned}\text{Gross profit margin} &= \text{Gross profit/Net sales} \\ &= \$323{,}000/\$760{,}000 \\ &= 0.425, \text{ or } 42.5\%\end{aligned}$$

Mal-Mart has $0.425 gross profit per dollar of sales. To improve the gross profit margin, Mal-Mart could raise the selling price of its products (if demand would not decrease) or reduce the cost of goods sold per dollar of sales.

■ The *EBIT margin* shows earnings before interest and taxes per dollar of net sales:

$$\begin{aligned}\text{EBIT margin} &= \text{Earnings before interest and taxes/Net sales} \\ &= \$171{,}000/\$760{,}000 \\ &= 0.225, \text{ or } 22.5\%\end{aligned}$$

Mal-Mart has $0.225 earnings before interest and taxes per dollar of sales. Since this ratio reflects factors affecting both gross profit margin and operating expense, a constant gross profit margin and a declining EBIT margin indicate a disproportionate rise in operating expenses.

■ The *before-tax profit margin* shows earnings before taxes per dollar of net sales:

$$\text{Before-tax profit margin} = \text{Earnings before taxes/Net Sales}$$
$$= \$134{,}000/\$760{,}000$$
$$= 0.176, \text{ or } 17.6\%$$

Mal-Mart has $0.176 in earnings before taxes per dollar of net sales.

■ The *after-tax profit* margin shows earnings after taxes per dollar of net sales:

$$\text{After-tax profit margin} = \text{Earnings after taxes/Net Sales}$$
$$= \$94{,}500/\$760{,}000$$
$$= 0.124, \text{ or } 12.4\%$$

Mal-Mart has $0.124 in earnings after taxes per dollar of net sales.

Two ratios related to profit margins are earnings per share (EPS) and dividends per share (DPS).

■ *Earnings per share* show earnings after taxes per share of common stock outstanding:

$$\text{Earnings per share} = \text{Earnings after taxes/Number of shares outstanding}$$
$$= \$94{,}500/50{,}000 \text{ shares}$$
$$= \$1.89$$

Mal-Mart has $1.89 in earnings after taxes per share of common stock outstanding.

■ *Dividends per share* are the amount of dividends paid to common shareholders on a per-share basis:

Dividends per share = Common dividends paid/Number of shares outstanding

Assume Mal-Mart paid $37,500 of the $94,500 in earnings after taxes as dividends to common stockholders:

$$\text{Dividends per share} = \$37{,}500/50{,}000 \text{ shares} = \$0.75$$

Mal-Mart pays $0.75 in dividends per share of common stock outstanding.

Chapter 13

Two variations of return on investment (ROI) are return on total assets (ROA) and return on common equity (ROE). Each measure combines data from the income statement with data from the balance sheet.

- *Return on total assets* measures the ratio of earnings after taxes to total assets:

$$\text{Return on total assets} = \text{Earnings after taxes/Total assets} \\ = \$94,500/\$645,000 \\ = 0.1465, \text{ or } 14.65\%$$

Mal-Mart earned $0.1465 per dollar invested in total assets. Return on total assets relates the shareholders' portion of sales revenues (earnings after taxes) to the resources both they and creditors contributed to the company (total assets equal total debt plus equity).

- A variation of ROA, the *earning power ratio*, measures earnings before interest and taxes per dollar of total assets:

$$\text{Earning power ratio} = \text{Earnings before interest and taxes/Total assets} \\ = \$171,000/\$645,000 \\ = 0.265, \text{ or } 26.5\%$$

This ratio shows the earning power of company assets independent of the way they were financed. Mal-Mart's assets earn $0.265 on the dollar before financing costs (interest) and taxes.

- From the shareholders' point of view, the most important ratio is *return on common equity*, which measures earnings after taxes per dollar of common equity:

$$\text{Return on equity} = \text{Earnings after taxes/Common equity} \\ = \$94,500/\$355,000 \\ = 0.266, \text{ or } 26.6\%$$

Mal-Mart earned $0.266 after taxes for each dollar of shareholder equity. A large return on equity attracts additional external equity capital, enables the retention of earnings, and makes possible large dividends.

- Return on equity is often called a return on book value because equity is measured as a book value rather than a market value. The market value counterpart to return on equity is *earnings yield*, which measures earnings per share divided by price per share:

$$\text{Earnings yield} = \text{Earnings per share/Stock price per share}$$

Suppose Mal-Mart's stock price is currently $12.00 per share:

$$\begin{aligned}\text{Earnings yield} &= \$1.89/\$12.00 \\ &= 0.158, \text{ or } 15.8\%\end{aligned}$$

Note that the reciprocal of the earnings yield is the price-earnings (P-E) ratio (stock price per share/earnings per share). Companies with a high stock price relative to earnings will have a high P-E ratio and a low earnings yield.

Asset management ratios measure the effectiveness with which management employs assets to generate sales revenue. Asset management ratios are called *turnover ratios*, net sales divided by a balance sheet item. A turnover ratio shows the sales revenue generated per dollar invested in assets.

- *Total asset turnover* is the most comprehensive measure of efficiency in using assets. It measures net sales per dollar of total assets:

$$\begin{aligned}\text{Total asset turnover} &= \text{Net sales/Total assets} \\ &= \$760,000/\$645,000 \\ &= 1.18\end{aligned}$$

Mal-Mart generated $1.18 in sales per dollar of total assets.

Large asset turnovers indicate that a company is using its total assets efficiently. An excessive investment in total assets decreases total asset turnover and reduces profitability ratios because of the costs associated with holding non-productive assets.

- The *current asset turnover* shows company sales revenue per dollar of current assets:

$$\begin{aligned}\text{Current asset turnover} &= \text{Net sales/Current assets} \\ &= \$760,000/\$340,000\end{aligned}$$

Chapter 13

$$= 2.24$$

Mal-Mart had $2.24 in net sales for each dollar of current assets.

■ The *accounts receivable turnover* measures credit sales per dollar of accounts receivable:

$$\begin{aligned}
\text{Accounts receivable turnover} &= \text{Credit sales/Accounts receivable} \\
&= (\$760{,}000 \times 0.93)/\$83{,}400 \\
&= \$706{,}800/\$83{,}400 \\
&= 8.47
\end{aligned}$$

Mal-Mart generated $8.47 in credit sales per dollar of accounts receivable.

When the mix of cash and credit sales is unknown, analysts use total sales in place of credit sales in calculating accounts receivable turnover.

■ *Average collection period (ACP)* is another ratio for evaluating the level of accounts receivable. ACP measures the average number of days it takes the company to collect accounts receivable:

$$\begin{aligned}
\text{Average collection period} &= \text{Accounts receivable/(Annual credit sales/365)} \\
&= \$83{,}400/(\$706{,}800/365) \\
&= \$83{,}400/\$1{,}936 \\
&= 43.1 \text{ days}
\end{aligned}$$

Alternatively, average collection period can be calculated using the accounts receivable turnover:

$$\begin{aligned}
\text{Average collection period} &= 365 \text{ days/Accounts receivable turnover} \\
&= 365/8.47 \\
&= 43.1 \text{ days}
\end{aligned}$$

It took Mal-Mart an average of 43.1 days to collect its accounts receivable.

Excessive investment in accounts receivable leads to a reduction in accounts receivable turnover, an increase in the average collection period, and a reduction in total asset turnover and profitability. Although stringent credit policies would result in a higher accounts receivable turnover and a shorter average collection period, care must be taken that the tightening of the credit policy does not come at the expense of lost sales.

- *Inventory turnover* measures a company's efficiency in using inventory and is indicated by the ratio of cost of goods sold to the level of inventory:

$$\begin{aligned} \text{Inventory turnover} &= \text{Cost of goods sold/Inventory} \\ &= \$437{,}000/\$110{,}000 \\ &= 3.97 \end{aligned}$$

Mal-Mart turns its inventory over 3.97 times per year; the company has $3.97 in sales, measured at cost, per dollar of inventory.

A low turnover relative to the industry average could be the result of (1) slow-moving inventory, (2) obsolete inventory, (3) spoiled inventory, or (4) too much inventory.

- *Days' sales in inventory* measures the average number of days required to sell inventory items:

$$\begin{aligned} \text{Days' sales in inventory} &= 365 \text{ days/Inventory turnover} \\ &= 365/3.97 \\ &= 91.9 \text{ days} \end{aligned}$$

It takes an average of 91.9 days to sell inventory items at Mal-Mart.

- The *fixed asset turnover* measures the company's sales per dollar of fixed assets:

$$\begin{aligned} \text{Fixed asset turnover} &= \text{Net sales/Net fixed assets} \\ &= \$760{,}000/\$305{,}000 \\ &= 2.49 \end{aligned}$$

Mal-Mart generates $2.49 in sales for each dollar invested in fixed assets.

The age of the company's fixed assets and the extent of leasing, in addition to differences in efficiency in the use of fixed assets, may cause the fixed asset turnover to differ among companies.

Chapter 13

Debt management ratios measure the way the company's assets are financed and the company's ability to service debt. Debt management ratios can be divided into two groups: (1) *debt ratios*, **measured with balance sheet data, and (2)** *coverage ratios*, **measured with income statement data.**

■ The *total debt ratio* measures the amount of total debt per dollar of total assets:

$$\begin{aligned}\text{Total debt ratio} &= \text{Total debt/Total assets} \\ &= \$290{,}000/\$645{,}000 \\ &= 0.45, \text{ or } 45\% \text{ debt}\end{aligned}$$

Mal-Mart has $0.45 total debt per dollar of total assets. Mal-Mart finances 45 percent of its total assets with debt.

■ The *debt-equity ratio* conveys the same information as the total debt ratio using a different format:

$$\begin{aligned}\text{Debt-equity ratio} &= \text{Total debt/Common equity} \\ &= \$290{,}000/\$355{,}000 \\ &= 0.82\end{aligned}$$

Mal-Mart's total debt is 0.82 times the size of its common equity, meaning the company has $0.82 total debt per dollar of common equity.

■ The *equity multiplier* is another alternative to the total debt ratio. It measures the dollar value of total assets per dollar of equity:

$$\begin{aligned}\text{Equity multiplier} &= \text{Total assets/Common equity} \\ &= \$645{,}000/\$355{,}000 \\ &= 1.82\end{aligned}$$

Mal-Mart's total assets are 1.82 times larger than its common equity, meaning that the company has $1.82 in assets per dollar of shareholder equity.

■ Because of the added refinancing risk of short-term debt, it should be analyzed separately from long-term debt. The *current debt ratio* measures current liabilities per dollar of total assets:

$$\text{Current debt ratio} = \text{Current liabilities/Total assets}$$
$$= \$106{,}000/\$645{,}000$$
$$= 0.164$$

Mal-Mart has $0.164 in current liabilities per dollar of total assets.

■ The *long-term debt ratio* measures long-term debt per dollar of total assets:

$$\text{Long-term debt ratio} = \text{Long-term debt/Total assets}$$
$$= \$184{,}000/\$645{,}000$$
$$= 0.285$$

Mal-Mart has $0.285 in long-term debt per dollar of total assets. The sum of the current debt and the long-term debt ratios equals the total debt ratio (0.164 + 0.285 = 0.449, or 0.45, rounded).

Coverage ratios contain only income statement items and refer to the number of times a company's earnings exceed its financing payments. Large ratio values mean that a company's earnings easily cover its payments.

■ The *times-interest-earned ratio* measures the coverage of interest expense:

$$\text{Times interest earned} = \text{EBIT/Interest Expense}$$
$$= \$171{,}000/\$37{,}000$$
$$= 4.62$$

Mal-Mart covered its interest expense 4.62 times during 1997; the company had $4.62 in EBIT per dollar of interest expense.

■ The *fixed charge coverage ratio* is a more comprehensive coverage measure in that it includes lease payments as a fixed financing charge:

Fixed charge coverage = (EBIT + Lease payments)/(Interest expense + Lease payments)

Chapter 13

Suppose Mal-Mart's operating expenses include $7,500 in lease payments:

$$\text{Fixed charge coverage} = (\$171{,}000 + \$7{,}500)/(\$37{,}000 + \$7{,}500)$$
$$= \$178{,}500/\$44{,}500$$
$$= 4.01$$

Mal-Mart covered its fixed charges 4.01 times in 1997; the company had $4.01 available to pay $1 of interest and lease payments.

■ These coverage ratios have two shortcomings: (1) They use earnings in the numerator instead of cash flow and (2) they ignore other fixed financing charges in the denominator. Some analysts use operating cash flow instead of earnings in the numerator to address the first problem. The second problem is sometimes addressed by adding principal repayments and preferred stock dividends (adjusted for taxes) to the denominator.

Liquidity ratios show a company's potential for paying its short-term and maturing long-term debt. Highly liquid companies have a large proportion of liquid assets compared with their current liabilities.

■ The *current ratio* measures current assets per dollar of current liabilities:

$$\text{Current ratio} = \text{Current assets/Current liabilities}$$
$$= \$340{,}000/\$106{,}000$$
$$= 3.21$$

At the end of 1997, Mal-Mart had $3.21 in current assets per dollar of current liabilities.

■ The *quick ratio*, also called the *acid test ratio*, recognizes that some current assets, such as inventory, are not as liquid as others. The quick ratio measures cash and near-cash assets per dollar of current liabilities:

$$\text{Quick ratio} = (\text{Current assets - Inventory})/\text{Current liabilities}$$
$$= (\$340{,}000 - \$110{,}000)/\$106{,}000$$
$$= 2.17$$

Mal-Mart's quick assets are 2.17 times its current liabilities; the company has $2.17 in quick assets for each dollar of current liabilities.

- In addition to checking a company's current and quick ratios, the analyst should check the company's cash balance and marketable securities to assure that the company has sufficient cash available to pay its bills.

There are two related models that bring together profitability, asset management, and debt management ratios: (1) The Du Pont model ties together profitability and asset management; (2) the extended Du Pont model ties together profitability, asset management, and debt management. Liquidity is handled outside of the models.

- The *Du Pont model* is an equation that breaks return on assets (ROA) into two determinant parts:

Return on total assets = After-tax profit margin × Total asset turnover

$$\frac{\text{Earnings after taxes}}{\text{Total assets}} = \frac{\text{Earnings after taxes}}{\text{Net sales}} \times \frac{\text{Net sales}}{\text{Total assets}}$$

$$= (\$94{,}500/\$760{,}000) \times (\$760{,}000/\$645{,}000)$$
$$= 0.124 \times 1.18$$
$$= 0.146, \text{ or } 14.6\%$$

Mal-Mart earns $0.146 after taxes for each dollar invested in total assets.

By breaking ROA into a profitability ratio and an asset management ratio, the Du Pont model enables a financial manager to find the reason for a company's low or high ROA.

- The *extended Du Pont model* adds the debt management dimension to the Du Pont model to calculate return on common equity (ROE):

Return on common equity = After-tax profit margin × Total asset turnover × Equity multiplier

Chapter 13

$$\frac{\text{Earnings after taxes}}{\text{Common equity}} = \frac{\text{Earnings after taxes}}{\text{Net sales}} \times \frac{\text{Net sales}}{\text{Total assets}} \times \frac{\text{Total Assets}}{\text{Common Equity}}$$

$$= \frac{\$94,500}{\$760,000} \times \frac{\$760,000}{\$645,000} \times \frac{\$645,000}{\$355,000}$$
$$= 0.124 \times 1.18 \times 1.82$$
$$= 0.266, \text{ or } 26.6\%$$

Mal-Mart earns $0.266 after taxes for each dollar of common equity. Note that return on assets (0.146) times the equity multiplier (1.82) also equals ROE (0.266).

By breaking ROE into a profitability ratio, an asset management ratio, and a debt management ratio, the model enables the financial manager to locate reasons for a company's high or low ROE.

A useful procedure for analyzing a company's financial statements consists of the following steps:

1. Review of the company's financial statements.
2. Application of the extended Du Pont model.
3. Assessment of the company's liquidity position.
4. Examination of the company's after-tax profit margins.
5. Examination of the current asset turnover and the fixed asset turnover, followed by the subsidiary turnovers.
6. Analysis of the equity multiplier and debt coverage ratios.
7. Interpretation of the findings, linking where possible the corroborating evidence from different financial ratios. This final step must be taken with care because managerial policies and accounting practices may cause financial ratios to appear to be something they are not.

Chapter 13

GLOSSARY OF KEY TERMS

after-tax profit margin: earnings after taxes per dollar of net sales

asset management ratios: ratios measuring sales per dollar invested in a specific type of asset

before-tax profit margin: earnings before taxes per dollar of net sales

common-size income statement: each value on an income statement expressed as a percentage of net sales

coverage ratio: earnings per dollar of financing payments

days' sales in inventory: average number of days required to sell inventory items

debt management ratios: ratios measuring the use of debt capital to finance assets

dividends per share (DPS): dividends paid to common shareholders on a per-share basis

Du Pont model: equation showing ROA as the profit margin times total asset turnover

earnings per share (EPS): earnings after taxes per share of common stock outstanding

earnings yield: earnings per share divided by price per share; reciprocal of the P-E ratio

EBIT margin: earnings before interest and taxes per dollar of net sales

equity multiplier: total assets per dollar invested (equity) by owners

extended Du Pont model: equation showing ROE as the profit margin times total asset turnover times the equity multiplier

fixed asset turnover: net sales per dollar of fixed assets

fixed charge coverage ratio: earnings available to pay fixed financing charges per dollar of fixed charges

floating interest rate: interest rate on debt changes (floats) with a specified market rate

gross profit margin: gross profit per dollar of net sales

industry comparative analysis: comparison of a company's financial ratios with industry average ratios

liquidity ratios: ratios measuring a company's potential for paying its bills

profit margin: profit per dollar of sales

profitability: dollar profit as a percentage of some other quantity

profitability ratios: ratios measuring profit relative to assets, equity, and sales

quick ratio: cash and near-cash assets per dollar of current liabilities

return on common equity (ROE): earnings after taxes per dollar of common equity

return on investment: profit per dollar of investment

times-interest-earned ratio: earnings before interest and taxes per dollar of interest expense

total asset turnover: net sales per dollar of total assets

total debt ratio: total debt per dollar of total assets

Chapter 13

trend analysis: interpretation of financial ratios displayed in time series

MULTIPLE CHOICE SELF-TEST

1. Financial ratios are used by

    a. financial managers to assess the operations of the entire company
    b. suppliers to judge a company's ability to meet short-term debts
    c. creditors who are concerned about the company's debt service ability
    d. shareholders in order to estimate the future performance of the price of common stock
    e. all of the above

2. Which of the following is true?

    a. Liquidity ratios measure the effectiveness of all managerial policies and decisions.
    b. Debt-management ratios measure the effectiveness with which management employs assets to generate sales revenue.
    c. Profitability ratios measure the company's ability to service debt.
    d. Asset management ratios show a company's potential for paying its short-term liabilities.
    e. none of the above

3. A comparison of the ratios of companies in the same industry

    a. underestimates borrowing power
    b. highlights managerial effectiveness
    c. emphasizes growth over time
    d. serves no useful purpose
    e. exaggerates profitability

Chapter 13

4. Return on total assets is a measure of

    a. equity management
    b. liquidity
    c. profitability
    d. opportunity
    e. variance

5. The most important profitability ratio to shareholders is

    a. return on equity
    b. earning power
    c. total asset turnover
    d. fixed cost coverage
    e. operating margin

6. The reciprocal of earnings yield is the

    a. loss yield ratio
    b. yield-earnings ratio
    c. debt-asset ratio
    d. price-earnings ratio
    e. asset-equity ratio

7. Asset management ratios are called _____ ratios.

    a. sales-asset
    b. profitability
    c. turnover
    d. margin
    e. coverage

Chapter 13

8. Accounts receivable turnover and _____ provide almost the same information.

    a. average collection period
    b. inventory turnover
    c. receivable holding costs
    d. credit margin
    e. payables turnover

9. Which of the following gives the dollar value of total assets per dollar of equity?

    a. total debt ratio
    b. total asset turnover
    c. return on equity
    d. equity multiplier
    e. after-tax profit margin

10. _____ ratios contain only income statement items and refer to the number of times a company's earnings exceed its financing payments.

    a. equity
    b. coverage
    c. liquidity
    d. turnover
    e. profitability

11. A company's potential for covering its current liabilities is shown by the

    a. accounts payable
    b. current ratio
    c. debt-equity ratio
    d. current profit margin
    e. retained earnings

Chapter 13

12. Which of the following ratios is improperly classified?

   a. equity multiplier = profitability ratio
   b. quick ratio = liquidity ratio
   c. fixed asset turnover = asset management ratio
   d. times-interest-earned = debt management ratio
   e. average collection period = asset management ratio

PROBLEMS

1. B. Cool, Inc. manufactures the Tru-Temp Thermostat. Bob Cool, CEO, reports annual thermostat sales of $17,000,000 and an after-tax profit margin of 14 percent. The company has 140,000 shares of common stock outstanding. Calculate B. Cool's earnings per share.

2. If B. Cool, Inc. in Problem 1 has total assets of $12,000,000 and an EBIT margin of 21 percent, what is the company's earning power ratio?

3. B. Cool's treasurer, Joe Cool, says the $75 market price of the company's common stock is equal to twice its book value. Using this fact and the data from the preceding two problems, calculate B. Cool's ROE.

4. Annual lease payments on B. Cool's production equipment equal $2,400,000. Based on the EBIT implied in Problem 2 and assuming B. Cool has zero interest expense, what is the company's fixed charge coverage ratio?

   Use the following information for Problems 5 through 8:

   The current financial records for Weight No More, Inc., operator of a chain of quick weight-loss clinics, were damaged by a fire. Weight No More's controller needs to reconstruct some figures for presentation at a board meeting this afternoon. The following information for the last calendar year is available:

Chapter 13

Shareholder equity	$500,000
Current liabilities	$250,000
Total assets	$900,000
Earnings per share	$2.50
Cost of goods sold	40 percent of total sales
Average collection period	30 days
Total asset turnover	2.5 times per year
Inventory turnover	6.75 times per year
Quick ratio	1.0
Marketable securities	zero
All sales are on credit	

5. What were Weight No More's net sales for the period?

6. Calculate Weight No More's accounts receivables for the period.

7. What is the balance in Weight No More's cash account?

8. Calculate Weight No More's investment in inventory.

9. Selected data from representative companies in three industries are given below:

	Retail Grocery	Electric Utility	Manufacturing
Sales	$1,500,000	$ 5,000,000	$3,500,000
After-tax earnings	$14,000	$800,000	$240,000
Total assets	$157,000	$12,000,000	$3,200,000
Common equity	$100,000	$5,500,000	$1,720,000

Using the extended Du Pont model, calculate the profit margin, total asset turnover, equity multiplier, and return on common equity for each company.

10. Comment on the different measures calculated for each company in Problem 9, especially on how each achieved its level of ROE.

Chapter 13

SOLUTIONS TO MULTIPLE CHOICE SELF-TEST

1. e
2. e
3. b
4. c
5. a
6. d

7. c
8. a
9. d
10. b
11. b
12. a

SOLUTIONS TO PROBLEMS

1. EPS = Earnings after taxes/Number of shares outstanding

   EAT = $17,000,000 × 0.14
       = $2,380,000

   EPS = $2,380,000/140,000
       = $17.00

2. Earning power ratio = EBIT/Total assets

   EBIT = $17,000,000 × 0.21
        = $3,570,000

   Earning power ratio = $3,570,000/$12,000,000
                      = 0.2975, or 29.75%

3. Return on equity = EAT/Common Equity

   Common equity = $75/2 × 140,000 shares
                 = $5,250,000

   Return on equity = $2,380,000/$5,250,000
                    = 0.453, or 45.3%

249

Chapter 13

4. Fixed charge coverage
   = (EBIT + Lease payments)/Interest expense + Lease payments
   = ($3,570,000 + $2,400,000)/($0 + $2,400,000)
   = $5,970,000/$2,400,000
   = 2.49

5. Total asset turnover = Net sales/Total assets
   2.5 = Net sales/$900,000
   Net sales = $2,250,000

6. Average collection period = AR/Daily credit sales
   AR = Daily credit sales × Average collection period
   Daily credit sales = $2,250,000/365
   = $6,164.38
   AR = $6,164.38 × 30
   = $184,931

7. Quick ratio = (Cash + AR)/Current liabilities
   1.0 = (Cash + $184,931)/$250,000
   $250,000 = Cash + $184,931
   Cash = $65,069

8. Inventory turnover = Cost of goods sold/Inventory
   Inventory = Cost of goods sold/Inventory turnover

   Cost of goods sold = $2,250,000 × 0.40
   = $900,000

   Inventory = $900,000/6.75
   Inventory = $133,333

9. The extended Du Pont model shows return on equity (ROE) as a function of three other ratios:

   Return on equity = Profit margin × Total asset turnover × Equity multiplier
   = (EAT/Sales) × (Sales/Assets) × (Assets/Equity)

Retail grocery:
   Profit margin = $14,000/$1,500,000 = 0.0093
   Total asset turnover = $1,500,000/$157,000 = 9.55
   Equity multiplier = $157,000/$100,000 = 1.57
   ROE = 0.0093 × 9.55 × 1.57 = 0.1394, or 13.94%

Electric utility:
   Profit margin = $800,000/$5,000,000 = 0.16
   Total asset turnover = $5,000,000/$12,500,000 = 0.40
   Equity multiplier = $12,000,000 /$5,500,000 = 2.18
   ROE = 0.16 × 0.40 × 2.18 = 0.1395, or 13.95%

Manufacturing:
   Profit margin = $240,000/$3,500,000 = 0.069
   Total asset turnover = $3,500,000/$3,200,000 = 1.09
   Equity multiplier = $3,200,000/$1,720,000 = 1.86
   ROE = 0.069 × 1.09 × 1.86 = 0.1399, or 13.99%

10. The three different companies all had an ROE of approximately 14 percent. That level of profitability was achieved, however, in quite different ways by each one.

The retail grocery company earned a net profit margin of less than 1 percent, but turned its assets over nearly 10 times during the year. The markup and margin in the grocery business are typically very low, and operating earnings depend on high sales volume.

In contrast, the electric utility company has a high profit margin, 16 percent, but an asset turnover ratio of only 0.4 times. To generate sales, utility companies require a large investment in fixed assets.

With a profit margin of about 7 percent and an asset turnover of about 1.1 times, the manufacturing company falls between the extremes of the grocery and utility companies.

While all three companies used debt financing to increase ROE, the utility had a larger equity multiplier than the other two. This is consistent with the nature of the large investment in fixed assets and the relatively greater predictability in the

Chapter 13

utility's revenue and operating costs.

14 FINANCIAL PLANNING

OVERVIEW

Much of a company's success in increasing shareholder wealth depends on how well the financial manager plans for company needs. Two financial planning methods, capital budgeting and developing cash budgets, were introduced in previous chapters. This chapter introduces two additional techniques -- percent-of-sales forecasting and break-even analysis. Sales forecasts are used for planning a company's requirements for external financing. Break-even analysis is used for planning profit levels of company investments.

OUTLINE

Forecasting future sales is the starting point for financial-planning models because sales affect the size of all other financial variables. Methods of forecasting sales include: (1) subjective forecasts, (2) trend forecasts, and (3) correlation forecasts.

- A *subjective forecast* develops expected sales based on personal experience and intuition, relying exclusively on the judgment of the person making the forecast. Advantages of the subjective forecast are that it is simple and inexpensive to implement, it draws upon the expertise of field personnel, and the person responsible for sales is making the forecast. Disadvantages include possible poor judgment of field personnel and over-reliance on recent sales experience.

  To refine subjective forecasts, management can use the *Delphi technique*, a process involving the use of a panel of experts who alternately present and modify their

Chapter 14

predictions until a consensus is reached.

- *Trend forecasts* are estimates of future sales based on past sales data. Trend forecasting is a time-series analysis that expresses sales as a function solely of time, typically, a number of years. Trend forecasts are usually more accurate when used for short-term forecasts (one year) than for longer periods because extrapolation from past sales may miss significant turning points in the long-run.

- *Correlation forecasts* can be used to relate past company sales to forecasts of macroeconomic variables. The accuracy of a correlation forecast depends on (1) the selection of an appropriate economic variable and (2) the accuracy of the forecast of that variable. Broad measures of economic activity, such as gross national product (GNP), are readily available, but often, a narrow measure of economic activity is a better predictor of a specific company's sales.

A forecast of increased sales leads to an expected increase in total assets to support the sales growth. An increase in assets necessitates increased financing from debt or equity sources.

- Armed with the forecast of increased sales, the financial manager's task is to estimate the increase in total assets and to plan the financing of the increase.

Percent-of-sales forecasting **is a method of forecasting the amount of external financing required because of growth in sales. Both the** *pro forma* **and equation methods of percent-of sales forecasting are based on the following relationship:**

The external financing required for a planning period will be equal to the total financing required less funds generated internally.

The *pro forma* method of percent-of-sales forecasting develops (1) an estimate of external financing required to support sales growth and (2) the resulting *pro forma* balance sheet and income statement. The first step in the *pro forma* method is a forecast of the increase in total assets expected as a result of an increase in sales, which will tell the financial manager how much total financing will be required.

- The increase in total assets depends on the company's *capital intensity ratio*, which measures the company's assets per dollar of sales and is the reciprocal of the total

254

asset turnover ratio. If a company's capital intensity ratio remains constant from one year to the next, the percentage change in assets will equal the percentage change in sales.

- For example, the E.Z. Rider Corporation (EZR), which manufactures farming equipment, had total assets at the end of the fiscal year of $320,450 and annual sales of $850,000. EZR's capital intensity ratio is:

$$\text{Assets/Sales} = \$320{,}450/\$850{,}000 = 0.377, \text{ or } 37.7\%$$

Suppose EZR has forecast a 12 percent increase in sales next year. If the capital intensity ratio remains constant, the percentage change in assets will be exactly the same as the percentage change in sales:

$$\begin{aligned}\text{Sales forecast} &= \text{Current sales} \times (1 + \text{growth rate}) \\ &= \$850{,}000 \times (1 + 0.12) \\ &= \$952{,}000\end{aligned}$$

$$\begin{aligned}\text{Assets next year} &= \text{Assets this year} \times (1 + \text{growth rate}) \\ &= \$320{,}450 \times (1 + 0.12) \\ &= \$358{,}904\end{aligned}$$

The *total financing required* by EZR to support the increase in sales is equal to the change in assets from one year to the next:

$$\$358{,}904 - \$320{,}450 = \$38{,}454 \text{ total financing required}$$

The second step in the *pro forma* method of percent-of-sales forecasting is to estimate the funds generated from internal sources.

- Internal sources of funds come from *spontaneous liabilities* and earnings retained during the year. Spontaneous liabilities arise from normal operations of the company and include accounts payable, taxes payable, and accrued wages. Spontaneous liabilities tend to rise proportionally with sales.

- For example, suppose total spontaneous liabilities (L) for EZR are $34,000 this year. Expressing L as a percentage of last year's sales (S) yields:

Chapter 14

$$L/S = \$34{,}000/\$850{,}000 = 0.04, \text{ or } 4.0\%$$

If L/S stays constant for EZR, total spontaneous liabilities for next year will be:

$$\$952{,}000 \times 0.04 = \$38{,}080$$

The expected increase in EZR's spontaneous liabilities next year is:

$$\$38{,}080 - \$34{,}000 = \$4{,}080$$

■ Retained earnings, the other source of internally generated financing, is equal to earnings after taxes (EAT) less dividends paid. If EZR has after-tax earnings equal to 3 percent of sales, and it pays 40 percent of earnings in dividends, earnings retained next year are estimated as:

$$\begin{aligned}
\text{Dividends} &= \text{EAT} \times \text{Dividend payout ratio} \\
&= (\$952{,}000 \times 0.03) \times 0.40 \\
&= \$28{,}560 \times 0.40 \\
&= \$11{,}424
\end{aligned}$$

$$\begin{aligned}
\text{Earnings retained} &= \$28{,}560 - \$11{,}424 \\
&= \$17{,}136
\end{aligned}$$

The third step in the *pro forma* method of percent-of-sales forecasting is to calculate the external financing required. External financing required is equal to total financing required less additional spontaneous liabilities and retained earnings.

■ For example, external financing required for EZR is:

Total financing required	$38,454
Less:	
Additional spontaneous liabilities	4,080
Earnings retained next year	17,136
External financing required	$17,238

EZR's financial manager will have to obtain $17,238 in external financing.

Chapter 14

Developing this external financing forecast gives the financial manager time to (1) analyze alternative sources of financing (debt vs. equity and short-term vs. long-term sources) and (2) arrange for advantageous financial terms. EZR's financial manager will use the estimated increases in assets and liabilities to construct a *pro forma* balance sheet for next year.

- Development of a *pro forma* income statement requires additional information on costs and expenses. Historical relationships between sales, cost of goods sold, and various operating expenses form the basis for the forecast of these items. Interest expense depends on outstanding debt and interest rates. Taxes are calculated with statutory rates.

Pro forma financial statements strengthen a company's applications for loans from financial institutions in addition to being useful in financial planning.

The equation method of percent-of-sales forecasting more directly estimates the external financing required by summarizing the *pro forma* method into a series of mathematical steps.

- If total assets (A) increase proportionally with sales (S), total additional financing required based on forecast sales (FS) is:

    Total financing required = (A/S) × (FS - S)

- Internal financing provided by increased spontaneous liabilities (L) is:

    Increase in spontaneous liabilities = (L/S) × (FS - S)

- Financing from retained earnings during a year is equal to earnings after taxes (EAT) less dividends paid (Div):

    Earnings retained during year = EAT - Div

- Combining the preceding three items yields the following equation for calculating external financing required (EFR):

Chapter 14

$$EFR = (A/S)(FS - S) - [(L/S)(FS - S) + (EAT - Div)]$$

■ For EZR, external financing required is:

$$(A/S) = \$320{,}450/\$850{,}000 = 0.377$$

$$(FS - S) = \$952{,}000 - \$850{,}000 = \$102{,}000$$

$$(L/S) = \$34{,}000/\$850{,}000 = 0.04$$

$$(EAT - Div) = \$28{,}56{,}0 - \$11{,}424 = \$17{,}136$$

$$\begin{aligned} EFR &= 0.377(\$102{,}000) - [0.04(\$102{,}000) + \$17{,}136] \\ &= \$38{,}454 - (\$4{,}080 + \$17{,}136) \\ &= \$38{,}454 - \$21{,}216 \\ &= \$17{,}238 \end{aligned}$$

■ Whether the financial manager should use the *pro forma* or the equation method of percent-of-sales forecasting depends on the purpose at hand. The *pro forma* method results in *pro forma* financial statements that are useful for financial planning and for presentation to creditors. The equation method is quicker and is particularly useful for analyzing the impact of changes in input values on external financing needs under different scenarios.

Break-even analysis is the process of forecasting the level of sales at which a company breaks even on its operations (before consideration of interest expense and taxes). At the break-even sales level, sales revenue equals total operating costs, and earnings before interest and taxes (EBIT) equals zero.

■ To calculate the break-even point, total operating costs must be broken into variable and fixed components so that:

Total sales revenue = Total variable costs + Total fixed costs

Sales revenue equals price per unit sold (P) times the quantity of units sold (Q). Variable costs are directly proportional to sales volume; therefore, total variable costs equal the variable cost per unit sold (V) times the quantity of units sold (Q). Fixed costs (F) are independent of the level of sales. Using these symbols in the above equation yields:

$$P \times Q = (V \times Q) + F$$

Solving for Q yields the break-even point in units (Q_B):

$$Q_B = F/(P - V)$$

The quantity (P - V) is the unit contribution margin. Total contribution margin equals (P - V)(Q). At the break-even point, total contribution margin is equal to the fixed costs of operations.

- The break-even point in sales revenue (S_B) is:

$$S_B = Q_B \times P$$

Alternatively, the break-even point in sales revenue can be calculated as:

$$S_B = F/[(P-V)/P] \quad \text{or} \quad S_B = F/[(S - TVC)/S]$$

In the first equation, (P - V)/P is the contribution margin ratio. In the second equation, TVC represents total variable costs and S is total sales revenue.

- For example, suppose that Pens To You (PTY) sells high quality felt-tip pens for $4.50 each. Variable production cost is $2.40 per pen and annual fixed operating costs are $126,000. PTY's unit contribution margin is:

Price per unit (P)	$4.50
Less variable cost per unit (V)	2.40
Unit contribution margin	$2.10

The break-even quantity of felt-tip pens is:

$$Q_B = \$126,000/\$2.10$$
$$= 60,000 \text{ pens}$$

Chapter 14

The break-even point in sales revenue is:

$$S_B = \$4.50 \text{ per pen} \times 60{,}000 \text{ pens}$$
$$= \$270{,}000$$

Alternately, S_B can be found as:

$$S_B = \$126{,}000/(\$2.10/\$4.50)$$
$$= \$270{,}000$$

The relationships among sales revenue, cost, and profit can be plotted on a graph illustrating the break-even point.

- Three steps are used to draw the graph:

  1. Draw a horizontal line representing fixed costs, which do not vary as sales volume changes.

  2. Draw the sales revenue line, using the origin and the break-even point as the two points for drawing the line.

  3. Draw the total operating cost line, using fixed costs at zero sales and the break-even point as the two points for drawing the line. Note that when sales are zero, the company still has fixed costs to pay; thus, the total cost line does not start at the origin but starts at the fixed cost line.

- The break-even point on the graph is the intersection of the sales revenue line and the total operating cost line. Production and sales volume lower than the break-even point result in a loss for the company. Production and sales volume above the break-even point result in positive earnings before interest and taxes for the company.

Break-even analysis is used by financial managers to analyze past performance and forecast future results.

- Financial managers can calculate the effects on the break-even point of changes in the input variables. For example, an increase in fixed costs leads to a higher break-even point. An increase in variable cost per unit also leads to a higher break-even point. An

Chapter 14

increase in the price per unit results in a lower break-even point. Of course, the price increase may cause a decrease in the quantity of the product demanded.

- Break-even analysis is used by company managers in several areas of planning and control. Financial managers use it in capital budgeting to supplement net present value analysis and in financing decisions to assess the company's ability to pay interest. Marketing managers use break-even analysis in product-pricing decisions, and production managers use it in operational decisions regarding automation.

Although break-even analysis generally assumes linear relationships, nonlinear analysis may more accurately describe the behavior of sales and total operating costs.

- Nonlinear break-even analysis allows for price reductions at high output levels and economies of scale in operating costs. In nonlinear analysis, sales revenue and total operating costs are drawn as curves and may result in more than one break-even point.

The use of fixed costs in a company's cost structure results in *leverage*, the power of a change in sales to change profit at a greater rate. Leverage stems from two aspects of a company's financial management -- its investments and its financing.

- *Operating leverage* arises from the use of fixed *operating* costs. Replacing labor with machines increases fixed operating costs and operating leverage. A percentage change in sales will result in a greater percentage change in EBIT when a company has operating leverage.

- *Financial leverage* arises from the use of fixed *financing* costs. Interest costs on debt or preferred-stock dividends are examples of fixed financing costs. Increases in fixed financing costs lead to increased financial leverage, so that a percentage change in EBIT will result in a greater percentage change in earnings after taxes.

The *degree of operating leverage (DOL)* measures the change in EBIT resulting from a change in sales:

DOL = Percentage change in EBIT/Percentage change in sales

- Determination of DOL involves the calculation of sales and the resulting EBIT at two

Chapter 14

different levels. For Pens To You (PTY), EBIT at a sales level of 75,000 pens is:

Sales (75,000 × $4.50)	$337,500
Less variable costs (75,000 × $2.40)	180,000
Contribution margin	$157,500
Less fixed operating costs	126,000
EBIT	$ 31,500

EBIT at a sales level of 82,500 pens is:

Sales (82,500 × $4.50)	$371,250
Less variable costs (82,500 × $2.40)	198,000
Contribution margin	$173,250
Less fixed operating costs	126,000
EBIT	$ 47,250

$$\text{Percentage increase in sales} = (\$371{,}250 - \$337{,}500)/\$337{,}500$$
$$= 0.10, \text{ or } 10\%$$

$$\text{Percentage increase in EBIT} = (\$47{,}250 - \$31{,}500)/\$31{,}500$$
$$= 0.50, \text{ or } 50\%$$

$$\text{DOL} = 50\%/10\%$$
$$= 5.0$$

Through the use of operating leverage, a 10 percent change in sales resulted in a 50 percent change in EBIT for PTY.

■ A more direct method of determining DOL is:

$$\text{DOL} = \text{Contribution margin/EBIT}$$

For PTY, DOL at 75,000 units is:

$$\text{DOL} = \$157{,}500/\$31{,}500 = 5.0$$

Chapter 14

The degree of operating leverage is different at each level of sales.

- At the break-even sales level, DOL is undefined because the contribution margin is divided by a zero EBIT. DOL is largest at sales levels near the break-even point and decreases as sales move away from the break-even point.

Increases in operating leverage increase *business risk*, the uncertainty of future earnings before interest and taxes.

- Uncertain future product prices and demand for products together with uncertain operating costs combine to create business risk. Adding operating leverage through fixed costs usually increases business risk even more.

The *degree of financial leverage (DFL)* measures the change in earnings after taxes (EAT) resulting from a change in EBIT:

DFL = Percentage change in EAT/Percentage change in EBIT

- If Pens To You (PTY) has interest expense of $9,300 and pays taxes at a 15 percent marginal rate, EAT at a sales level of 75,000 pens is:

EBIT	$31,500
Less interest expense	9,300
EBT	$22,200
Less taxes (0.15)	3,330
EAT	$18,870

EAT at a sales level of 82,500 pens is:

EBIT	$47,250
Less interest expense	9,300
EBT	$37,950
Less taxes (0.15)	5,693
EAT	$32,257

Percentage increase in EBIT = ($47,250 - $31,500)/$31,500
= 0.50, or 50%

Chapter 14

$$\text{Percentage increase in EAT} = (\$32{,}257 - \$18{,}870)/\$18{,}870$$
$$= 0.71, \text{ or } 71\%$$
$$\text{DFL} = 71\%/50\%$$
$$= 1.42$$

Through the use of financial leverage, a 50 percent increase in EBIT led to a 71% increase in EAT. Stated differently, a ten percent increase in EBIT would result in a 14.2 percent increase in EAT.

■ A more direct method of determining DFL is:

$$\text{DFL} = \text{EBIT/EBT}$$

For PTY, the DFL at 75,000 units is:

$$\text{DFL} = \$31{,}500/\$22{,}200$$
$$= 1.42$$

Using fixed-cost debt instead of common stock to raise capital increases a company's *financial risk***, the uncertainty of a company's future earnings after taxes.**

■ Fixed interest cost is only one cause of financial risk. All of the factors that cause business risk also add to the uncertainty of earnings after taxes. For this reason, financial managers of companies with large business risk typically prefer to use small amounts of financial leverage to minimize the uncertainty of future earnings after taxes.

The *degree of combined leverage (DCL)* **measures the change in earnings after taxes resulting from a change in sales. It combines the effects of operating leverage and financial leverage together in one measure:**

$$\text{DCL} = \text{Percentage change in EAT/Percentage change in sales}$$

■ For PTY, the DCL at a sales level of 75,000 pens is:

$$\text{DCL} = 71\%/10\%$$
$$= 7.1$$

Chapter 14

Through the use of combined operating and financial leverage, a 10 percent increase in sales would lead to a 71 percent increase in EAT.

■ A more direct method of calculating DCL is:

$$DCL = DOL \times DFL$$

For PTY, DCL is:
$$DCL = 5 \times 1.422$$
$$= 7.1$$

■ In summary, operating and financial leverage combine to widen the swings in earnings after taxes resulting from any change in sales. The nature of a company's products and the production methods in the industry largely determine the mix of variable and fixed operating costs, making it difficult to change the company's degree of operating leverage. The amount of financial leverage the company should have depends largely on the stability of its sales. Companies with stable product demand and low operating leverage can afford to use more debt financing than companies with unstable product demand and large operating leverage.

GLOSSARY OF KEY TERMS

break-even analysis: analysis of the relationship among sales revenue, operating costs, and profits; at the break-even point, sales revenue equals total operating costs and EBIT = 0

capital intensity ratio: assets per dollar of sales; reciprocal of the total asset turnover ratio

correlation forecast: statistical forecast based on the systematic link between the forecast variable and one or more other variables

degree of combined leverage: measure of the change in earnings after taxes resulting from a change in sales

degree of financial leverage (DFL): measure of the change in earnings after taxes resulting from a change in EBIT

Chapter 14

degree of operating leverage (DOL): measure of the change in EBIT resulting from a change in sales

Delphi technique: process of modifying the subjective forecast of each person on a panel to derive a consensus forecast

external financing required: funds raised outside of a company to support growth; total financing required less internal sources of funds

leverage: power of a change in sales to change profit at a greater rate

percent-of-sales forecasting: forecasting a company's external financing required because of growth in sales

spontaneous liabilities: costless short-term debt that arises in the normal course of company operations

subjective forecast: forecast of expected values using personal experience and intuition

total financing required: required increase in total debt and equity associated with increases in assets and sales

trend forecast: forecast based on historical data arrayed in order of time

MULTIPLE CHOICE SELF-TEST

1. Which of the following is not part of financial planning?

    a. break-even analysis
    b. capital budgeting
    c. developing cash budgets
    d. percent-of-sales forecasting
    e. all of the above are part of financial planning

2. Trend forecasts are based on

    a. future sales expectations
    b. past sales data
    c. the current fashion
    d. gross national product
    e. interpolation

Chapter 14

3. The purpose of percent-of-sales forecasting is to determine

   a. expected sales based on subjective forecasts
   b. the break-even point in units
   c. expected sales based on trend analysis
   d. a company's external financing requirements because of growth in sales
   e. expected sales based on correlation forecasting

4. The capital intensity ratio measures

   a. sales per dollar of assets
   b. assets per dollar of sales
   c. EBIT per dollar of sales
   d. EAT per dollar of sales
   e. EAT per dollar of EBIT

5. Internal sources of financing include

   a. spontaneous liabilities and new common stock
   b. retained earnings and long-term debt
   c. dividends and operating income
   d. retained earnings and spontaneous liabilities
   e. earnings after taxes and depreciation

6. Spontaneous liabilities include all of the following except

   a. accounts payable
   b. accrued wages
   c. notes payable
   d. taxes payable
   e. all of the above are spontaneous liabilities

Chapter 14

7. At the break-even point

    a. EBIT equals total sales
    b. EAT equals EBIT
    c. total sales equal total fixed costs
    d. total fixed costs equal total variable costs
    e. total sales equal total operating costs

8. On a graph illustrating the break-even point, the total fixed cost curve is a(n)

    a. upward-sloping line
    b. downward-sloping line
    c. horizontal line
    d. vertical line
    e. none of the above

9. Break-even analysis is useful in

    a. capital budgeting
    b. financing decisions
    c. product pricing
    d. operational decisions
    e. all of the above

10. The power of a change in sales to change profit at a greater rate is called

    a. leverage
    b. economies of scale
    c. capital intensity
    d. Delphi technique
    e. correlation

Chapter 14

11. If a company automates production, the likely result is to

    a. raise the break-even point
    b. decrease profitability
    c. change the degree of financial leverage
    d. reduce fixed operating costs
    e. increase DFL

12. DCL measures

    a. the change in earnings after taxes resulting from a change in EBIT
    b. the change in earnings before interest and taxes resulting from a change in sales
    c. the change in earnings after taxes resulting from a change in sales
    d. the change in total financing required
    e. the change in external financing required

PROBLEMS

1. Scientific Methods, Inc. (SMI) had net sales of $250,000 in 1997 and total assets at the end of the year of $70,000. Sales for SMI are forecast to increase by 15 percent for 1998, but the capital intensity ratio will remain unchanged. SMI's spontaneous liabilities were $20,000 in 1997; they are expected to increase proportionally with sales. Retained earnings for 1998 are expected to be $5,300. Calculate the amount of external financing required for 1998.

2. Your company's sales are expected to increase by 8 percent in the coming period. Sales for the past year were $375,000. The ratio of assets to sales is 0.45, the ratio of spontaneous liabilities to sales is 0.06, and the company earns 2.5 percent after taxes on sales. None of these ratios is expected to change. The company policy is to pay 30 percent of earnings as dividends. Calculate the amount of external financing required for the coming period.

3. When Quality Chemicals increased its sales from $800,000 to $1,000,000, earnings before interest and taxes went from $15,000 to $20,000 for the same period. What is Quality Chemicals' DOL?

Chapter 14

Use the following information for Problems 4, 5, and 6:

Best Boxes, Inc. has the following operating statement for the year ended December 31, 1997:

Sales (5,000 units @ $150 each)		$750,000
Less variable costs		
Materials and supplies	$250,000	
Wages and utilities	150,000	400,000
Contribution margin		$350,000
Less fixed operating costs		250,000
Operating profit (EBIT)		$100,000
Less interest		30,000
Earnings before taxes		$ 70,000
Less taxes (34%)		$ 23,800
Earnings after taxes		$ 46,200

4. What is Best Boxes' break-even point in units and in dollars?

5. If variable costs increase by 15 percent, what level of sales is required to maintain the same EBIT? What is the revised break-even point in units?

6. Calculate the company's degree of combined leverage at 5,000 units sold.

SOLUTIONS TO MULTIPLE CHOICE SELF-TEST

1. e   7. e
2. b   8. c
3. d   9. e
4. b   10. a
5. d   11. a
6. c   12. c

Chapter 14

SOLUTIONS TO PROBLEMS

1. Change in assets = $70,000 × 0.15
   = $10,500
   Change in spontaneous liabilities = $20,000 × 0.15
   = $3,000
   External financing required = $10,500 - $3,000 - $5,300
   = $2,200

2. Change in assets = $375,000 × 0.08 × 0.45
   = $13,500
   Change in spontaneous liabilities = ($375,000 × 0.08) × 0.06
   = $1,800
   Retained earnings = ($375,000 × 1.08) × 0.025 × 0.70
   = $7,087.50

   External financing required = $13,500 - $1,800 - $7,087.50
   = $4,612.50

3. % change in sales = ($1,000,000 - $800,000)/$800,000
   = 0.25

   % change in EBIT = ($20,000 - $15,000)/$15,000
   = 0.33

   DOL = % change in EBIT/% change in sales
   = 0.33/0.25
   = 1.32

4. Variable cost per unit = Total variable cost/Sales quantity
   = $400,000/5,000
   = $80

   Q_B = F/(P - V)
   = $250,000/($150 - $80)
   = 3,571.43, or 3,572 units

$$S_B = Q_B \times P$$
$$= 3{,}572 \times \$150$$
$$= \$535{,}800$$

5. Increased level of TVC = $\$400{,}000 \times 1.15$
   $= \$460{,}000$

   EBIT = Sales revenue - Total costs
   EBIT = S - (TVC + F)
   $\quad$ S = EBIT + TVC + F
   $\quad\quad$ = \$100,000 + \$460,000 + \$250,000
   $\quad\quad$ = \$810,000

   Revised Q_B = \$810,000/\$150
   $\quad\quad$ = 5,400 units

6. DOL = Contribution margin/EBIT
   $\quad\quad$ = \$350,000/\$100,000
   $\quad\quad$ = 3.5

   DFL = EBIT/EBT
   $\quad\quad$ = \$100,000/\$70,000
   $\quad\quad$ = 1.43

   DCL = DOL × DFL
   $\quad\quad$ = 3.5 × 1.43
   $\quad\quad$ = 5.0

For each 1 percent change in sales revenue, EBIT changes 3.5 percent. For each 1 percent change in EBIT, EAT changes 1.43 percent. Thus, for each 1 percent change in sales revenue, EAT changes 5 percent.

15 INTERNATIONAL FINANCIAL MANAGEMENT

OVERVIEW

The basic principles of financial management apply to international as well as domestic operations. However, when operating in an international environment, additional factors must be considered. Any company buying or selling goods and services abroad deals with foreign currency, which is traded in foreign-exchange markets. This chapter discusses the different types of foreign-exchange markets, foreign-exchange rates, and sources of financing for multinational businesses. Companies that invest abroad and obtain financing from foreign sources must be prepared for the risks unique in foreign business. Three types of risk -- social, political, and foreign-exchange -- and various strategies companies can employ to reduce exposure to foreign-exchange risk are explored.

OUTLINE

Foreign currency is bought and sold in foreign-exchange markets. There are three different types of foreign-exchange markets:

- The *spot market*, also called the cash market, is the market for immediate delivery of foreign currencies. This market is used whenever financial managers need foreign currency for immediate payment.

- The *forward market* is a network of banks that write tailor-made contracts to sell or buy a negotiated amount of foreign currency for delivery in the future at a price set

Chapter 15

today. The forward market offers flexibility in the size of the contract and the date of delivery.

- The *futures market* is a centralized trading facility in which standardized contracts trade for future delivery of foreign currency. The contracts have standardized maturity dates and are written for standardized monetary amounts.

Financial managers normally use the forward market when they expect actual delivery of the currency to occur. They normally use the futures market for hedging risk.

A foreign-exchange rate is the number of currency units of one country needed to buy the currency unit of another country. Foreign-exchange rates are determined by the supply of and demand for foreign currency in foreign-exchange markets.

- An increase in demand for a foreign currency may be related to a number of different factors: (1) an increase in imports by other countries of the foreign country's products, (2) increased tourist travel to the foreign country, (3) multinational companies' expansion of facilities located in the foreign country, and (4) increases in foreign aid and military assistance to the foreign country.

- The increase in demand for a foreign currency causes its price to increase. An increase in the price of foreign currency means that it *appreciates* in relation to the home currency. When the foreign currency appreciates, the home currency is said to *depreciate*. Depreciation is the decrease in price of one currency in relation to another.

The financial press presents daily quotations of foreign-exchange rates.

- Foreign-exchange quotations are expressed in *American terms* as the U.S. dollar cost of foreign currency. The quotations are expressed in *European terms* as the amount of foreign currency per U.S. dollar.

- International transactions are sometimes expressed in terms of a collection of currencies. An SDR is a special drawing right originally developed by the International Monetary Fund. An ECU is a European currency unit, an average value of the currencies of countries in the European Community.

The quotations show the spot rate for each currency and forward rates for several

Chapter 15

actively traded currencies.

- The forward rate is an unbiased forecast of the future spot rate. A forward exchange rate below the spot exchange rate is a *forward discount*, suggesting a lower future spot rate and a weak currency. A forward rate above the spot rate is a *forward premium*, indicating a higher future spot rate and a strong currency.

When transacting business in international markets, companies use alternatives to the domestic methods of short-term financing.

- A draft is an order written by an exporter, or seller, requesting the importer, or buyer, to pay a specified amount of money on a specified date. If the importer agrees to pay the draft, the draft is a *trade draft*. If the importer's bank agrees to pay the draft, it is a *bank draft*.

  Trade and bank drafts may be one of two types. A *sight draft* is payable upon presentation. A *time draft* is payable on a future date.

  When an importer accepts a time draft, it becomes a *trade acceptance*; when the importer's bank accepts a time draft, it becomes a *banker's acceptance*. The acceptance is returned to the exporter, who may hold it until maturity or sell it at a discount from face value.

- Another form of short-term financing is a bank loan denominated in foreign currency. The source of these loans is *Eurocurrency*, currency held outside its country of origin. Eurocurrency loans are often made with a floating interest rate tied to LIBOR. LIBOR is the interest rate at which London banks loan Eurodollars to each other.

U.S. companies may issue stock in a foreign country as long as they conform to the regulations of the country.

- *The Wall Street Journal* reports selected stock prices daily on exchanges in London, Frankfurt, Milan, Sydney, Toronto, and Tokyo. Each exchange establishes its own set of requirements and fees for listing.

- U.S. companies issue common stock less frequently than bonds in foreign countries. Because foreign companies typically pay out a high percentage of earnings in

Chapter 15

dividends, U.S. companies issuing shares in these markets are pressured to do the same to attract investors. Additionally, overseas equity markets are not as liquid as U.S. equity markets, making it more costly to raise large sums of capital.

U.S. companies often use foreign markets to issue bonds.

- *Eurobonds* are bonds issued outside the country in whose currency the interest and principal are paid. U.S. companies issue about 40 percent of their bonds in the Eurobond market. About half of the Eurobond issues have floating rates based on LIBOR.

- Companies also issue *foreign bonds*. A foreign bond is a bond issued in a country foreign to the issuer and denominated in the foreign country's currency.

- Eurobonds offer benefits in comparison with foreign bonds. Uncertainty surrounding future exchange rates is eliminated with Eurobonds since interest and principal are paid in the issuer's home currency. The Eurobond market is much larger and can accommodate larger issues than the foreign-bond market. Additionally, the Eurobond market is largely unregulated, reducing flotation costs and the time required to issue a Eurobond. Finally, Eurobonds are usually in bearer form, providing anonymity to investors.

Transacting international business subjects a company to three types of risk: (1) social, (2) political, and (3) foreign-exchange risk.

- *Social risk* is the uncertainty of future cash flows as a result of different laws, languages, and business customs.

- *Political risk* is the uncertainty of future cash flows as a result of a country's sovereign power. The possibility that assets may be expropriated (seized) by a foreign sovereign power creates political risk.

- *Foreign-exchange risk* is the uncertainty of future cash flows arising from unexpected changes in foreign-exchange rates.

A multinational company faces three types of foreign-exchange risk: (1) translation, (2) economic, and (3) transaction risk. Translation risk arises from the translation of foreign-currency-denominated values into the company's home currency.

Chapter 15

- When companies translate and present in their financial statements the results of foreign operations denominated in foreign currency, they recognize foreign currency gains or losses depending on whether the foreign currency has appreciated or depreciated. The change in foreign-exchange rates during a reporting period affects assets and liabilities and may cause net worth to change.

- If the foreign currency appreciates, the foreign-currency-denominated assets rise in domestic-currency value, leading to a *translation gain*. Foreign-currency-denominated liabilities also rise in domestic-currency value, leading to a *translation loss*.

- Depreciation of the foreign currency leads to a translation loss on assets and a translation gain on liabilities, reported on the parent company's financial statements.

Economic risk is the uncertainty in operating cash flows of foreign operations resulting from *unexpected* changes in exchange rates. Economic risk is a long-term problem that a company addresses by making adjustments in its foreign production and marketing strategies.

- To reduce exposure to economic risk, a company might: (1) locate a new plant in the foreign country, (2) increase advertising for its products to increase sales, (3) market products targeted toward high-income, less price-sensitive customers, and (4) reduce costs by altering production processes. Each of these steps requires a commitment of large expenditures.

Transaction risk results from an unexpected change in foreign-exchange rates between the time that a transaction occurs and the time that payment is made. Transaction risk is a short-term phenomenon.

- Companies cope with transaction risk by adjusting credit terms, collection policy and payment policy. Exporting companies use credit and collection strategies to minimize transaction risk, and importing companies use payment strategies.

- Liberal credit terms are granted to customers whose currencies are likely to appreciate. Customers whose currencies are likely to depreciate are given strict credit terms.

- Collections from customers whose currencies are weak are accelerated, while collections are relaxed for customers whose currencies are strong.

Chapter 15

- Payments to suppliers whose currencies are strong are accelerated. A company may even consider paying cash. Payments to suppliers whose currencies are weak are delayed.

- In addition to adjusting credit and payment policies, companies also adjust prices to nullify the effect of varying foreign-exchange rates. Companies often increase the resale price of imported products to compensate for appreciation of foreign currency.

To reduce risk from uncertain exchange rates further, many companies use hedging techniques.

- A company can use the forward (or futures) market to establish a position opposite to the currency position in the spot market. A company expecting to receive payment in foreign currency hedges in the forward market by contracting with a bank to deliver foreign currency. A company expecting to make a payment in foreign currency hedges by contracting with a bank to accept delivery of foreign currency.

Capital budgeting for a foreign project is a two-step process: (1) Calculate the present value of the project's cash flows at the affiliate's required rate of return, and (2) calculate the present value of cash distributed from the affiliate to the parent company at the parent company's required rate of return.

- The foreign affiliate estimates the incremental cash flows from the foreign project. These cash flows are discounted at the affiliate's required rate of return. The affiliate's capital-budgeting committee accepts projects with positive net present values and rejects those with negative net present values.

- The amount and timing of project cash flows to be distributed from the affiliate to the parent company are then estimated. Foreign-denominated cash flows are translated into home currency at expected future exchange rates. Incremental home-currency-denominated cash flows are discounted at the parent company's required rate of return to find the net present value. Only projects with positive net present values from the parent company's point of view are accepted.

Social risk, political risk, and foreign-exchange risk factors must be taken into account when planning for capital investments in a multinational company.

Chapter 15

GLOSSARY OF KEY TERMS

appreciation: increase in the price (often measured in U.S. dollars) of foreign currency

depreciation: decrease in the price (often measured in U.S. dollars) of foreign currency

economic risk: foreign-exchange risk arising from changes in operating cash flows from foreign operations

Eurobond: bond issued outside the country in whose currency the interest and principal are paid

Eurocurrency: currency held outside its country of origin

foreign bond: bond issued in a country foreign to the issuer and denominated in the foreign country's currency

foreign-exchange rate: number of currency units of one country needed to buy the currency unit of another country; the price of foreign currency

foreign-exchange risk: uncertainty of future cash flows arising from unexpected changes in foreign-exchange rates

forward discount: forward exchange rate below the spot rate, indicating a weak currency

forward market: network of banks that write tailor-made contracts for future delivery of foreign currencies

forward premium: forward exchange rate above the spot rate, indicating a strong currency

futures market: centralized trading facility in which standardized contracts trade for future delivery of foreign currency

multinational company: company with operations in more than one country

political risk: uncertainty of future cash flows as a result of a country's sovereign power

sight draft: draft payable upon presentation by the exporter to the importer

social risk: uncertainty of future cash flows as a result of different laws, languages, and customs

spot market: market in which foreign currencies trade for immediate delivery; cash market

time draft: draft payable on a future date

transaction risk: foreign-exchange risk arising from settling a transaction in foreign currency

translation risk: foreign-exchange risk arising from the translation of foreign-currency-denominated values in to the company's home currency

Chapter 15

MULTIPLE CHOICE SELF-TEST

1. Foreign currencies are bought and sold in the

   a. Eurobond market
   b. multinational market
   c. foreign-exchange market
   d. international trade market
   e. New York Stock Exchange

2. The price of foreign currencies

   a. is set once a day by the International Monetary Fund
   b. changes each hour on the London Stock Exchange
   c. is always the same in all markets
   d. generally declines over time
   e. changes continually each day

3. A(n) _____ currency is one for which the forward rate is below the spot rate.

   a. weak
   b. undervalued
   c. strong
   d. overvalued
   e. volatile

4. A forward discount on a currency

   a. exists when the forward rate exceeds the futures rate
   b. may be caused by heavy selling in the forward market in anticipation of a decline in the spot rate
   c. may be caused by heavy buying in the forward market in anticipation of an increase in the spot rate
   d. indicates that a currency is strong
   e. indicates that the country issuing that currency has very low interest rates

Chapter 15

5. U.S. dollars deposited in a London bank are called

   a. English dollars
   b. European currency units (ECUs)
   c. special drawing rights (SDRs)
   d. Eurodollars
   e. LIBORs

6. A Eurobond is any bond

   a. issued in the U.S. by a U.S. company that is traded in European markets
   b. issued in a European country
   c. issued outside the country in whose currency the interest and principal are paid
   d. that has a lower interest rate than a comparable U.S. bond
   e. any bond traded on a European exchange

7. Dollar-denominated bonds issued in the U.S. by a Japanese company are called

   a. Eurobonds
   b. foreign bonds
   c. international bonds
   d. Asian bonds
   e. none of the above

8. Compared with the foreign bond market, the Eurobond market

   a. is much larger
   b. requires more time for issuance
   c. is more regulated
   d. is used less by U.S. companies
   e. is farther away

Chapter 15

9. Translation risk arises from

   a. purchasing foreign currencies for use in the futures market
   b. difficulty in interpreting exchange rates listed in foreign newspapers
   c. the translation of foreign-currency-denominated operations into the company's home currency
   d. managers who cannot speak the language of an international affiliate
   e. difficulty in calculating U.S. dollar equivalents of foreign currencies

10. Economic risk and transaction risk differ primarily in the

    a. size of their impact
    b. time period of their impact
    c. accounting treatment
    d. country of origin
    e. relation to translation risk

11. A U.S. multinational company can reduce transaction risk by

    a. requiring payment in U.S. dollars
    b. paying and receiving cash at the time of purchase or sale
    c. adjusting credit terms and payment policies
    d. hedging in the forward or futures markets
    e. all of the above

12. The purpose of hedging a currency transaction is to

    a. reduce economic risk
    b. reduce equivalency risk
    c. reduce translation risk
    d. reduce transaction risk
    e. reduce transportation risk

Chapter 15

13. A British company must pay a U.S. company $500,000 in three months. How can the British company reduce its exchange-rate risk?

   a. sell dollars in the spot market
   b. buy dollars in the forward market
   c. sell dollars in the forward market
   d. buy pounds in the forward market
   e. sell pounds in the forward market

14. Differences between capital-budgeting procedures for a domestic investment and a foreign investment include the need to consider

   a. the greater uncertainty in expected cash flows to the home country due to exchange-rate changes
   b. the possible expropriation of assets
   c. the greater risk of management mistakes due to unfamiliarity with foreign cultures and language
   d. differences in tax rates and rules
   e. all of the above

PROBLEMS

1. The spot rate for the Swedish krona is $0.1304 and the spot rate for the Greek drachma is $0.004521. How many Swedish krona will it take to purchase one Greek drachma?

Use the following information for Problems 2 through 5:

Foreign Imports, Inc. imports Japanese cars from Miklassa Motors for 160,000 yen each and sells them for $20,000 each. The yen is worth $0.10 in the spot market and $0.09 in the 90-day forward market.

2. What does each car cost Foreign Imports in U.S. dollars at the spot yen price?

Chapter 15

3. If Foreign Imports pays for its cars on 90-day credit, can it save any money on the cost of each car? If so, how much?

4. If Foreign Imports does not purchase the yen for 90 days, how much does each car cost in U.S. dollars if the spot market price is then $0.12?

5. How much does Miklassa receive for each car in Japanese yen if the value of the yen decreases to $0.08?

Use the following information for Problems 6 and 7:

Multinational Conglomeration Corporation (MCC) has assets and liabilities denominated in Deutsche marks: DM450,000 in assets and DM240,000 in liabilities. The exchange rate between U.S. dollars and Deutsche marks is $1.00 = DM2.00.

6. Calculate MCC's net translation gain or loss if the Deutsche mark appreciates against the U.S. dollar by 20 percent.

7. MCC will receive a payment of DM500,000 from a customer in 90 days. The forward rate of the Deutsche mark is $1.00 = DM2.10. What should the company do to protect against a possible transaction loss?

SOLUTIONS TO MULTIPLE CHOICE SELF-TEST

1. c	8. a
2. e	9. c
3. a	10. b
4. b	11. e
5. d	12. d
6. c	13. b
7. b	14. e

Chapter 15

SOLUTIONS TO PROBLEMS

1. 1 krona = $0.1304
    1 dollar = $1.00/$0.1304 = 7.6687 krona
    1 drachma = $0.004521
    1 dollar = $1.00/$0.004521 = 221.19 drachma
    1 dollar = 7.6687 krona = 221.19 drachma
    1 drachma = 7.6687/221.19 = 0.03467 krona

2. 160,000 yen × $0.10 = $16,000

3. Yes. If Foreign Imports purchases 160,000 yen in the 90-day forward market, it will save $0.01 per yen, or $1,600.

4. 160,000 yen × $0.12 = $19,200

5. Miklassa receives the same 160,000 yen per car regardless of the exchange rate fluctuation because Foreign Imports is paying in yen.

6. Before appreciation: 1 DM = $1.00/DM2.00 = $0.50
    After appreciation: 1 DM = $0.50 × 1.20 = $0.60

Change in value of assets:	
Value after appreciation (DM450,000 × $0.60)	$270,000
Value before appreciation (DM450,000 × $0.50)	225,000
Translation gain on assets	$ 45,000
Change in value of liabilities:	
Value after appreciation (DM240,000 × $0.60)	$144,000
Value before appreciation (DM240,000 × $0.50)	120,000
Translation loss on liabilities	$ 24,000

    Net translation gain = $45,000 - $24,000 = $21,000

Chapter 15

7. Since MCC is *receiving* marks in the future, a hedge against a change in the value of the mark would involve *selling* a contract in the forward market for an equivalent amount.

   The mark costs $1.00/DM2.10, or $0.47619. Therefore, the contract will be to deliver DM500,000, and MCC will receive $238,095 (DM500,000 × $0.47619), excluding transaction costs.